Pilton P

Past and Present
in their own words (mostly)

"Remembering with a Chuckle"

1952-2012

Edited by Jenny de Gex

CONTENTS

First published in 2012
Conkers Editions, Hyde House, Pilton, Somerset BA4 4BY
(jennydegex@btinternet.com)

Foreword, linking texts and compilation ©Jenny de Gex

Front cover calligraphy by Malcolm Drake

Design and layout by Gail & George Milne

ISBN 978-0-9572611-1-2

Front cover photo ©Jason Bryant
Back cover photo ©Ian Sumner

Printed and bound by Remous Limited, Milborne Port, Dorset DT9 5EP

ACKNOWLEDGEMENTS

Thanks first and foremost to the editorial team of Liz Elkin and Sandra Howe, for invaluable historical input, without whom this would have been impossible. Between us we made suggestions and brought in contributions. Thanks also to Gail Milne for design, George Milne for technical assistance with the images and not least to Kelly Sumner for underwriting this project, which was, after all, partly his suggestion.

Thanks to all contributors or those who have helped in any way, great or small, to put this together, with apologies for any unintentional omissions:

Sheelagh Allen, Hilary Austin, Katheryn Austin, Candace Bahouth, Tony Bailey, Scott Baldwin, Ron Ballantine, Jasmine Barker, John Barkle, Hugh Berry, Martin Berkeley, Christopher Bond, John Boucher, John Boyce, Robin Cade, Daphne Cannock, Fiona & Mike Case, Margaret & Jim Cellan-Jones, Leonora Clarke, David Cornwell (John Le Carré), James Crowden, Maurice Davies, Neil Davies, Jean & Ken Dilkes, Jim Dowling, Malcolm Drake, Margaret Drew, Michael Eavis, Philip Eavis, Ruth Eavis, Liz Elkin, Sukey Erland, Annie Fewlass, John Fletcher, Verona Fraser-Mackenzie, Judith Freane, Molly Gingell, Sally & Grant Goldie, Vivien Goode, Eileen & Jim Govier, Camille Greacen, Sue Green, Carolyn Griffiths, Linda Heathcoat-Amory, Pauline Hobbs, Robert House, Sandra & John Howe, Charles Johnson, Rob Kearle, Guy Kennaway, Andrew Kerr, Chris & Joe King, Kate Lewis, Rue Losey, Ray Loxton, Jeannie McNeill, Angela McPherson, Emma Macdonald, Mid Somerset News and Media (Emma Frampton, Oliver Hulme, Fran Weelen), Margaret Miles, Ann Millard, Suzanne Millard, Gail & George Milne, Totty Milne, Angela Morley, Tod Morris-Adams, David Osborne, Charlie Pearce, Pilton Village History Society, Ada Plumley, Janet & Richard Raynsford, Remous Ltd (Keith Sparks), Ashley Robertson, Jim Rogers, Bob Scanlon, Claire Steadman, Sheila Steward, Alan Stone, Kelly Sumner, Fred Swingler, Eileen Taylor, Maureen & Steve Tofts, Shannon Turner, Kate & Stephen Turner, Tim Walker, Fay Weldon, Dan Weldon, Sheila West

Grateful thanks to the following for permission to use extracts from copyright material:

©Janet Coward for *Barn Owl* poem 1939 by her father John Jarmain from *Collected Poems*, Collins 1945 ©Estate of John Jarmain 1945, ©Andrew Kerr, *Incredibly Hip, The Memoirs of Andrew Kerr*, Frontier Publishing 2011, ©Alan Stone *In Search of Cider*, 2012, www.somersethistory.co.uk, ©Shannon Turner for the late Douglas Turner's *Five Farms, A Somerset Farmer's Life*, 2005

FOREWORD

When the idea of compiling memories or anecdotes over the last 60 years to mark the Diamond Jubilee was first raised at a Jubilee Committee meeting, we never expected to end up with such a rich and varied miscellany. Kelly Sumner said he "wanted to know where all the best conker trees and apple orchards and the old shops were." These and much else besides you will discover, although several people think different places the best!

This collection of reminiscences is the tip of an iceberg, the result of a bright idea of "doing something for the Jubilee," inevitably constrained by deadline and pages. Although contributors were initially reluctant, once the ball started rolling, we found we were inundated with suggestions.

Although three of us threw ideas around and contacted people, for which I have to thank Liz Elkin and Sandra Howe for their continued support, it fell to me to pull everything together. Wherever possible, contributors' own words have been used but the linking texts and comments are mine, in italics, so I can only apologise for any errors. Every attempt has been made to check names and dates but memories, by definition, can be slightly hazy and there may well be omissions or inaccuracies.

Gathered here – and from others who have moved on – is a great deal of talent. Some of the contributions are by professional writers, poets, artists and photographers who have all freely donated their work, which remains their copyright, as do all the contributions. As I wrote in Roundabout, it is a community project, not-for-profit and privately sponsored.

Planned as a celebration, you will find little sadness or scandal, thus not totally true to life (as Rev David Osborne pointed out). It's mainly upbeat and light-hearted. The compilation cannot hope to be comprehensive but gives a taster of how life has changed. It has been fascinating to put together and I can only marvel at the detail of some people's memories. With such a wealth of activities, not all village organisations are featured but if ever there is a reprint, we would welcome new anecdotes for inclusion.

What follows on these pages is an arbitrary mixture, aiming to paint a picture of the contrasts of a community, tracing the progressions of the last half century or so. It was only in the 1960s that mains drainage came to the village.

A village was not considered a true village unless it had a pub, a shop, a garage. Recently I went through the phone book begun by my parents when they moved here: it had all of those plus a local policeman and a real telephone number to speak to a human being at the nearest train station. The telephone exchange then still only had three numbers (Pilton XXX) so one imagined someone sitting plugging in wires, as in old black and white films. Now it's Broadband and Wi-Fi for all but no shop, no garage: how fast things have changed.

Since 1970 the Festival is threaded throughout: it is a separate story of its own, well chronicled elsewhere but this attempts to factually record a balanced view, showing its effect on the village, coming through the bad years to its current separate well-managed city. From 1,500 people then, to selling out 170,000 tickets for 2013 in an hour and twenty minutes, plus being six times voted the best festival in the world, is a major achievement for a Somerset farmer.

There is – and has been over the years – so much talent in this small community. There is also generosity of spirit: many unsung heroes work tirelessly at every village event. This enthusiasm for a special place we all love generates an atmosphere of goodwill and good humour. It is this spirit of community and kindness that we hope these few pages will convey: despite the speed and pressures of modern life, it can and does continue.

The second Elizabethan reign is now almost as long as Queen Victoria's, duly celebrated at national and local levels. This book was therefore planned to commemorate the many changes seen over the 20th and 21st centuries as people recalled, before memory fades.

Hopefully it will come across in the intended spirit: to look back on events, occasions and people, remembering with warmth and affection and a smile of recognition, accompanied by a chuckle or two. Many of the best stories we were told were unprintable but I hope there is enough here to "remember with a chuckle."

Jenny de Gex, Pilton, October 2012

INTRODUCTION

Prince of Wales passing through Pilton 1909

Levi Rodgers butchers

Girl Guides 1930

Williams Stores, Crown Inn

And Did Those Feet?

Legends have abounded for centuries around the Vale of Avalon, mostly the creation of clerics, academics or authors, boosting the pilgrimage or tourist trade. In the early 20th century, Prebendary Bennett came to Pilton and popularised his own versions, as John Fletcher recounts:

Prebendary Bennett was vicar of Pilton from 1899 until 1934 and possibly the world's first Glastafarian. At a time when there were no NHS or pensions, Uncle Charlie, as he was affectionately known, did his best to nurse the sick and lame by providing them for free with herbal remedies he grew in his garden. Like many vicars at that time it was also his duty to provide some sort of food and shelter for those without.

But Uncle Charlie also held strong religious beliefs. He was a member of an organisation called the British Israelites. They believed (and still believe: the world headquarters is in County Durham for some reason) that one of the Twelve Lost Tribes of Israel wandered all round the continent before ending up in Britain. They even believed the royal family are descended from King David. We are thus the direct descendants of Abraham and Noah *et al*.

Uncle Charlie, Prebendary Bennett

This connection between Israel and Britain began centuries earlier when, allegedly, Joseph of Arimathea, uncle of Jesus and a trader, turned up in Glastonbury with the 12 year old Jesus to buy some Mendip-mined lead from us Ancient Britons. After the Crucifixion of Christ, he returned to Glastonbury to bury the Holy Grail. Interest in these matters seems to have been particularly intense in Prebendary Bennett's time: in 1906 two sisters, friends of Wellesley Tudor Pole, founder of the Chalice Well Trust, happened to rediscover a mysterious cup, later claimed to be the Holy Grail, in a drainage ditch behind Morland's Leather Factory, known as Bride's Well following the Celtic Revival. This caused a stir in the press, even at national level, from 1907 onwards.

But Uncle Charlie, as a true Piltonian, wasn't going to put up with any rubbish about Joseph of Arimathea and Jesus visiting *Glastonbury!* Why would they put up with tatty crystal shops and mystical paraphernalia when they could enjoy the true splendours and glories of Pilton and book very advanced tickets for the first pop festival? It was to celebrate their visit that he dedicated the Lady Chapel in the Church to Joseph of Arimathea. And he wrote a play explaining it all, *The History of Our Race*, which was performed in the 1930s in front of packed and enthusiastic audiences in Pilton church.

1

All that may or may not be true. But don't let us believe that this inter-parochial chauvinism and competitiveness on where Joseph and Jesus may or may not have visited existed just between Glastonbury and Pilton. West Compton got in on the act as well.

I remember standing with Owen Boyce, a farmer, in a field of his in West Compton in the 1970s. We were talking about this and that, and then Owen, as natural and gentle a Blakeian mystic as you'd ever meet, casually observed that his grandparents, who'd presumably been around in the 1860s or so, had once seen Joseph and the Christ Child walking along the footpath which ran on the opposite side of the field we were in. Despite his historical sense of time seeming slightly out, he vehemently affirmed they had seen them and showed me the exact spot where they'd trod.

So those feet, in Ancient Times, really did walk on England's green and pleasant land, even if it was only West Compton.

Pilton First Church, Harbour, Britons, & huts as they were probably seen from Cumhill about A.D. 50, with King Arviragus & Joseph of Arimathea.

A postcard illustrating Uncle Charlie's vision of Pooltown

The idea of Pilton being a harbour, as the name theoretically derives from Pooltown, continued in village history written by a more recent Vicar, Rev John Walker but is now dismissed by local historians. The name is cited elsewhere as deriving from the Saxon pyl *or* Pil *meaning a stream or creek and* tun *meaning a settlement or farm.*

In true West Country tradition, Methodism was strong in the village. The first Preaching House here, for which the Chapel still have the deeds, was built in 1794, which Philip Eavis stresses: is a very, very early date for a Methodist Meeting House. It was built by various business people from outside the village, where Jubilee House is now, along from the Chapel. Very interesting deeds, as to what they should and shouldn't do. The present Chapel was built in an orchard of that same one in 1849. That was a Wesleyan Chapel. The primitive Methodist Chapel was at Ebenezer.

The Chapel also organised outings: this historic photo from 1928 shows members of the Connock, Eavis, Hiscox and Norris families on a charabanc outing

The Litten family, seated in the back row, he with a long white beard, lived at Hyde House until 1929 and Donald, one of the grandsons, came to visit in the 1990s and shared some of his memories, as did a cousin, Agnes Coats, who knew Edith Hiscox. Agnes's mother was a Stacey:

I used to come on happy holidays, Christmas, Easter, for my father worked in Bristol. My grandmother's father was a cobbler who went to Australia during the Gold Rush, not to dig gold but to mend the boots of the gold diggers. He made £2,000 and bought the house in 1894: in his will he donated the property, a housekeeper and an income to my grandmother, his only daughter (my father's mother). Although my grandfather had been a real poverty-struck man, as a lay preacher, he travelled for Blackie & Son and suddenly became a gentleman

3

farmer. He peddled antiques from Shepton Mallet market, taking along eggs, fruit that they grew here, to trade for beautiful tables, chests, chairs. I can remember going in a horse and cart on his journeys in the early '20s: what fills me with nostalgia is that, aged four, I first found cowslips growing by the thousand by that hedge.

My naughty brothers used to leap from the upper bedroom into the yew hedge with their hands outstretched. There was an orchard next door. Grandma grew nectarines up the walls, as well as strawberries. There used to be strawberry teas for the whole village. I remember hiding under the hedge when a gyrocopter came over (before helicopters). There was a greenhouse full of geraniums, a lovely smell. We had to get our water from a well.

All the cousins gathered for Christmas, there'd be 18-20 people: Grandpa would have the carving knife. Little glass lamps were up the stairs as we went to bed, opening one eye to see Santa Claus: I saw my mother stuffing in those pink sweet mice and oranges.

Grandpa was a massive man with a beard and a large smile: he'd sit in a huge wicker chair, with two sticks, full of rheumatism. He said he knew rhubarb wasn't good for him but he wouldn't be told what to do, he made up his own mind. Health caught up with them, they became almost unable to move. So the house went out of the family, sold for £2,500.

In Prebendary Bennett's day, there were two butchers, three bakers, three shops, including a Post Office, a village policeman, a nurse, a blacksmith, a shoemender, three carpenters and three pubs: The Crown, Barrow Stile Pub and The Bush.

The brewery behind the Post Office used to make cider and later became Bill Appleby's carpentry workshop

The Bush was a pub until the 1950s, one of three in the village

In papers lodged with the Village History Society, Reg Green, Sue's father, describes how:

Before I left school, when I was about 8 years old, I used to go into the cornfields, rook scaring, carrying wooden clappers to scare birds off the corn, from 6am to 10pm. I earned 2 shillings a week. Farm labourers' wages then were 12 shillings a week. As I got older, I started to work with the horses with my father, who showed me how to become a good carter. I learnt ploughing, drilling, mowing etc and eventually took over the horses on my own. Then came the tractor....

Gertie with lamb

...Two fishmongers came from Shepton Mallet with pony and cart, one was 'Curly Case' (otherwise known as 'Fishy') and the other Mr Lumber. The oil man, Mr Dunkerton, used to come from Shepton and buy rabbit and mole skins. George the Pop man used to walk from Shepton, pushing a trolley and sold sweets, cotton and oddments. Gertie Barnard, the Post Lady, used to walk to deliver letters to Steanbow, North Wootton, Westholme and Redlake every day and sometimes she'd bring her pet lamb with her at 7.30am.

The grandson of John Beale, not of the Hill (that John was his grandfather's uncle) but of the Dell, and son of Muriel Beale, Mr C.S.B. Smith lodged his childhood memories with the Village History Society in 1990:

From about 1927 to 1934, my mother Muriel E. Beale, used to take us to spend a summer holiday with our grandparents at the Dell. We usually stayed for two or three weeks and then moved on to Burnham, where father would join us. We arrived by train, and were collected from West Pennard station by Mr Guppy, also the postman, in his Morris Six taxi.

We three children slept together in a large feather bed; it was very cosy to sink deep into the feathers. The bedroom door, and most of the others, had little semi-circular openings cut out at the bottom, to allow cats to run in and out to catch any mice, but we never saw any, although no cat was kept.

For washing there was a jug and basin on a washstand. The water was cold from the pump (above a well) in the washhouse beside the stream. Drinking water was brought from the tap in the recess in the wall in Shop Lane opposite the east end of the Church, and the day's supply was kept in two galvanised buckets in the kitchen.

All our visits were made in summer, so the big range in the living room was never alight, and all cooking was done on a two-burner paraffin stove. All lighting was by means of paraffin lamps or candles but I rarely saw them, being in bed before they were lit.

Baths were taken in a hip bath in the washhouse. We didn't look forward to them very much, as it was a very cold room with a stone floor and a north window, and the small amount of hot water, heated in saucepans, did not create much warmth. Much more fun was to put the large washing tub in the yard on a warm sunny day, and splash about in it after the water had been allowed to warm up for an hour or two.

The washhouse also contained a large iron mangle with wooden rollers, and a knife board and bath brick. I believe that the latter was made from Bridgwater silt, and a little was scraped on to the board to clean the steel knives once a week. Grandfather also had a barrel of cider there.

Near the washhouse on the bank of the stream was the privy, a long seat with two holes, one large and one small. It was very spidery and in those days they were very large indeed. A visit after dark with a candle was quite terrifying! Beneath the privy was a cesspit, from which there must have been a small opening into the stream, so the contents would gradually disintegrate, as no sewage was ever seen in the stream, where water was always clear and sparkling as it ran over the pebbles.

Before breakfast, I would go with Grandfather to Cumhill Farm with a quart can to get it filled with milk, warm from the cow, milked while we waited. There was a stone stile, and a footpath leading from the bottom of Cumhill up to the farm. Grandfather only had one arm, but it must have been very strong, as he held a spade or fork with it, and cultivated the large garden, winning a silver cup for the best-kept garden in Pilton.

Muriel Beale's wedding 1920

We children were rather fascinated by a heavy wooden egg cup which he used, shaped rather like an inverted pudding basin with a deep cavity in the top for the egg. He did not shave, but had closely trimmed whiskers, which he kept short with scissors in the stable every few days. Also in the stable was an old milk churn containing maize, or Indian corn, we called it, for the hens; it was not used for human consumption. The hens also had a hot meal every day, as Grandmother would boil up the small or marked potatoes and other substandard vegetables for them.

At harvest time, large wooden rakes about eight feet wide were drawn by horses to gather up the straw; we watched this being done in the field to the west of the Tithe Barn.

We also enjoyed playing in the pool at the base of the weir in the stream along Barrows, past Dover Cottage.

Margaret Windsor (née Harvey) was born in 1919 and came to Pilton aged 7 all the way from North Wootton, living first beside the Ford, in one of two cottages later knocked together, forming Barrow House. The following incident happened at Cedar Cottage, soon before the family moved to the Crown:

We used to have a bath in one of these oval-shaped baths and we always had to heat the water in the old-fashioned copper, and to heat the water we used to burn newspapers, old shoes, any old rags, anything to heat the water, because coal, although very cheap wasn't cheap because you didn't have the wages in

Margaret Windsor in 1938, aged 19

those days. And then my father and my brother would be sent out and we four girls would have a bath in the same water in front of the one and only fireplace. When I was about 15 or 16 we had what they called the 'Bungalow bath'; it was about four foot long and you could stretch your legs out. Well then, when you got to that age, it was time to have a bath in the back kitchen and the only heat you had was the little bit of heat from the fire under the copper. In fact our back

King George VI Coronation in May 1937
L to R- Gertie Watch, Mrs Cleeves,
Harriet Plumley, Ethel Pearce.

kitchen was half underground, so you can guess how cold it was in there. The bolt was outside not inside, so when you had a bath, someone would lock the door. Now the larder was on one end of this long narrow back kitchen, and one Saturday afternoon, I suppose I was 17, I was there sat in this bath and the bolt shot back and who walked in but the butcher! Can you imagine it! I couldn't stand up, I couldn't do anything. But he said "Hello, Margo," walked straight in, put the meat in the larder – in those days we had a cover that went over to keep the flies off of it because there were no fridges, no electricity – and he put this thing over the meat, shut the larder door, said "Cheerio, Margo," locked the door and that was that. I felt dreadful. You think of being 17 and having the butcher walk in when you were in the bath!

A writer later known for his war poetry, who also wrote fine poems inspired by nature and landscape, briefly lived in Pilton from 1935 until the outbreak of war. First married to an artist, Evelyn Houghton, he subsequently married Beryl Butler, whose uncle Reg Lawton lived at The Cedars and worked for United Dairies. In common with subsequent writers who lived here, he earned his crust teaching at Millfield, founded in 1935 by the legendary R.J.O. Meyer. Jarmain also lived at West Pennard in the early 1930s but it is thought the poem below, entitled Barn Owl *dating from August 1939, refers to a Pilton owl. A rarer sight perhaps today, thus one to treasure.*

Great soft wings, pale and creamy-yellow,
Downy-soft and silent, with long sleepy beat
Slow and lazy-moving in the haze of summer evenings
When silence like a curtain ends the day's long heat;

Fat fluffed-up body with the tiny bones inside it.
Skeleton no bigger than a child's small hand;
Tiny body hidden in the fluffed downy feathers
Slowly sailing, skimming the dusk still land;

Hedge-high he sails with flapping noiseless wing-beats,
Hunts the lines of stubble ready for the plough;
Slowly turns and slowly rises, as if he were too heavy,
Upward planes, and settles on a low elm bough.

In the same silent evenings years ahead in other summers,
When our eyes have drunk the quietness that time passed yields,
Still the owl will fly there, the same one or another,
Big and softly sailing in these or other fields;

Will float hedge-high, hunt the lines of stubble,
With slow flapping flight along the warm dusk air;
And you and I will stand there together in the doorway,
Saying to each other, "Look, the old owl's there."

Jarmain was killed in 1943 fighting in France, having survived the Battle of El Alamein and was with the 51st Highland Division as part of the 8th Army invasion of Sicily. He had a premonition of death in the first line of a poem written in June 1939, Thinking of War, echoing Rupert Brooke:
  "If I must die, forget these hands of mine..."

The 'Shepton Mallet Journal' recently published a 'Yesteryear' piece about Mr & Mrs George Rose who were married in 1902 and celebrated their Diamond Wedding in 1962, saying he built the first brick house in Pilton. He said There was strong feeling at the time, because the majority of houses in the village were built of local stone. The oldest brick house would appear to be Hill Rise on Shop Lane. His son, Charles, father of Colin, took over his building firm.

Alb 'Cocker' Pearce c1933

John Pearce, Alb's son, with car outside Culverwell Cottages where they moved in 1938

Gould's Garage in 1939, with bicycles outside and the Pilton name taken down to confuse the enemy

The outbreak of war in 1939 changed life for everyone. In May and June 1940, volunteers joined the Home Guard, of which Pilton had a Platoon, as did West Pennard. Fortunately they were never put to the test but nonetheless trained and did everything 'properly' and not as per haystack-and-pitchfork mythology. Jim Rogers remembers how it was:

Unlike the accepted view of Dad's Army, the Pilton Home Guard boasted several young men. Mr Dew had served in WW1 and, as an experienced serviceman, he was in charge of our patrol.

Pilton Home Guard, from left: Sgt. Bert Dew, Jim Rogers, George Windsor, Alf Dew, Jack Harris, Eddie Harris, Alec Green, Bill Appleby

We went for training at the Searchlight Battery, situated along Park track at the bottom of Park Hill. Here we were taught to march and fire a rifle. We became able to move as a unit rather than as individuals milling about. All the men had a rifle but I manned the Lewis gun and George Windsor was my observer.

We met in the early evening at HQ, a hut off the road to the left of Burford Cross. We patrolled along the ridge from the top of Stoodley Hill to the junction with the A361. It was a good viewpoint as we could see much of the village and also watch the anti-aircraft flak over Bristol. A few bombs were dropped on Pilton but the only casualties were animals.

When we finished our patrol at about 6am I went straight to work in the bakery with my father. It was an exciting time for a young man.

The Women's Land Army worked at Steanbow, then a farm run under the War Ag scheme and at the Tithe Barn, where a commemorative stone seat made by stonemason Phil Thomason was placed in 2006, unveiled at a reunion of surviving Land Girls, with much reminiscing and laughter.

Stanley Williams painting of Land Girls, done from memory, 1961

Ada Plumley, on the left in the photo, remembers what it was like, as she came here as a Land Girl in 1947, having already been evacuated from Liverpool to South Wales for the war years. Like several others, she stayed in Pilton, marrying Ken Plumley. They returned to Liverpool for 40 years, before retiring to Pilton in the 1990s. He was *the* "only banana ripener in Liverpool." *She and Fay Fleming are the only surviving Land Girls living here today.* We were taught hand milking but I had already tried this, as I learned when I was evacuated to South Wales with my brother. I came to Steanbow when I was 18. I don't think I ever used a machine for milking.

A lot of girls came there that didn't know anything at all. I remember one girl and she couldn't touch the cow! Every time she went near a cow she went all funny, she couldn't touch the udders or anything, she'd go to pieces.

A few years ago, we all got our Land Army badges which was a crest and certificates. I was going down to Steanbow to be photographed by the same door but it's been changed now.

Ada Plumley at Steanbow as a Land Girl

Keith Johnson, whose family home was in Surrey, lived in wartime with his maternal grandparents in Twerton, before visiting Pilton because his two aunts, Dolly and Ethel had joined the Land Army:

Italian Prisoners of War also worked for the War Ag scheme at Cumhill, shown here in 1943 with Patrick Eavis, Charlie Pearce, Ray Langridge together with Mrs Brooks, of Cumhill

Dolly, who later settled in Pilton, worked on market gardens in Surrey, whilst Ethel came to Steanbow where she did some milking by hand. She also specialised in driving tractors and reaper binders and later American combine harvesters.

On the 19th February my mother and I visited Steanbow and stayed with Joe and Long Ede Green, the parents of Reg Green, who on 20th February 1944 became my uncle as he married my aunt Ethel.

My abiding memory of those days around the wedding is of Somerset humour laced with plenty of cider and I recall the scandalized astonishment of Pilton locals when my maternal grandfather, a strict teetotaller, refused a pint of farmhouse cider.

"Dussent drink cider – wa's drink then?"

"Yer, he don't drink cider"

Unbelievable was the verdict.

Mother and I returned to Surrey until Hitler, who was intent on stopping me growing up, dropped a doodlebug close to our Surrey home, and so we returned to the safety of Steanbow where I spent the glorious summer of 1944, and I helped defeat Hitler by carrying sheaves to make the corn stooks. There was a really happy atmosphere at Steanbow amongst everybody who worked there, no doubt encouraged by the success of the invasion backed up by the huge aerial armada of planes that literally filled the sky, heading towards France and contributing to Nazi downfall.

Evacuee children were sent out of London to escape the Blitz and later described their memories of Pilton. Alf Cockram was billeted at the Manor:

When I was seven years of age and my brother Bill was nine, my mum and dad were told that we would have to be evacuated to the country because of The Blitz. It was 1940.

We were taken by train to Shepton Mallet and then on to the village of Pilton. When we arrived all the evacuees were assembled in the playground of Pilton Village School to await selection. We all stood with our name tags pinned to our coats and carrying anything our parents were allowed to give us in satchels. Then a group of ladies from the village started to choose the evacuees they wanted billeted with them. My brother and I were picked by a woman in a Red Cross nurse's uniform, she also chose a little girl. We were then driven off to what would be our home for the next four years.

As we first drove up to The Manor House we thought it was very daunting and didn't know what to expect. When we entered the house we were met by the husband of the Red Cross nurse, Mr Franklin Wheaton-Smith, they were both American. We were later told that he was profoundly deaf and we had to learn sign language. He was a nice man and very kind to us. Later on we were introduced to the staff: Joyce Thompson the cook. Bill Laye the butler, Frank Stockwell Snr and Frank Jnr, who were the gardeners.

The Wheaton-Smiths had a grown-up daughter and son. Their daughter, Barbara, lived in America. The son, Major Craig, was an officer in the army and married to Princess Tatiana Wiasemsky, who was something to do with the Selfridges family. Bill and I were pageboys at their wedding in St Martin in the Fields in London. Despite the war being on, the family still managed to entertain quite a lot and we met many interesting people. I recall meeting Julian Huxley, Professor Joad and A. J. P. Taylor.

Mr and Mrs Wheaton-Smith lived in the house for the duration of the war. Bill and I occupied a room over the dining room, which faced onto the lawn. We always got back before dark as we were told the house was haunted! Apparently, a ghostly aristocratic lady had been seen in the driveway getting out of a coach and horses. I have to say we never saw anything. The little girl who was billeted with us only stayed for a couple of weeks, as she missed her brothers who had been sent to another home but we never knew what happened to her.

The grounds of the Manor seemed enormous to us, bearing in mind our home in London was just two rooms. Our village life was very different from London and it took some time to ease our way into the ways of the village. We became choirboys at St John the Baptist church and met Revd Harold Hughes. We were confirmed by him in 1943. Our days in Pilton Village School were good, as we took more nature walks than lessons in the classroom! We would play and wander around the village, so the locals got to know us and, eventually, we were accepted.

During the summer, we used to help with the harvesting, along with the Land Army girls and the Italian POWs camped at West Pennard. We also had lots of fun pole-vaulting across the steam with Fido, our Highland Terrier. We didn't always make it to the other side and fell in many times but became quite proficient in the end.

My brother went back to London in 1944, when he was 12 years old. I went back a year later when I was 11. As we grew up we would reminisce about our days at The Manor House and realised we were very lucky little boys to be picked that day.

Pilton Village School, founded in the 1890s was going strong in the 1940s and reunions held in 2008 and 2011 brought together many former pupils from those days. Margaret Miles has less flattering memories of school dinners, in a piece entitled The Pit and the Playground:

School dinners! And Pilton school dinners were probably no worse and no better than anywhere else in the country. However, they were vastly different from today's well-cooked meals, which as far as I know are catered to give pupils a choice of menu and diets. There was no choice back in the '40s, no diets worked out for vegetarians or diabetics, you got what you were given, and however horrible it was, you ate it. On one occasion, I was eating some prunes and custard when my spoon came up with a 'prune' that was incredibly hard, a little too round and attached to a long silvery chain! Hauling it out from the gooey custard, it turned out to be a sink plug which some short-sighted dinner lady had mistaken for a prune!

But even more gruesome than this were the stews. I'm talking about plates of almost pure grease, lumped about with grey vegetables and unchewable meat swimming in gravy the colour of dirty washing-up water. That meat was so tough that even the Komodo dragons, who can eat everything except cement, couldn't have got their teeth into it. Certainly none of us could and that was the problem, because our headmistress, a kindly but strict lady, made us eat *everything.* So we devised a plan, because we knew she kept everyone at the dinner table until they'd finished these revolting meals, even if, as usually happened, a crust of congealed fat had covered the top. You were made to stay at table until every morsel had gone. I remember two boys, evacuees living on a farm at Burford, found by their hosts still sitting over plates of disgusting stew at 6.30pm, watched over by the headmistress.

Our plan was this: we would, sometime during the meal, pretend to cough or sneeze, so we could slip the meat from our mouths into our hankies, the boys quickly shoving theirs into pockets, the girls hiding theirs in knicker legs. Later, out in the playground, we sneaked away to the pit, a dim, almost dark place where large mounds of anthracite and coal were kept and, when we were pretty sure no one was looking, we threw the bits of meat over the low wall, before strolling innocently back to the playground. And no one was any the wiser, or so we thought.

Someone was, of course, hell-bent on being teacher's pet, a girl. She saw one of the boys throw some lumps of meat into the pit and straightaway told the headmistress. As soon as the head appeared in the playground, our small group sensed trouble. Loudly and sternly she gathered us together. She immediately began to question Robert about the meat, and knowing he had been well and truly caught, he could do nothing but admit it, before apologising and saying he wouldn't do it again. He probably thought he'd get a telling-off and that would be the end of it. If only things were that simple. She then ordered him to climb over the low pit wall and retrieve the lumps of meat he had thrown in. How could he do that, I wondered, since the pit was as black as your hat down near the ground, besides, others had thrown stuff in there and there were probably rats and mice running about, so how could he be sure he'd find *his* bits of meat? Of course he couldn't and he knew this as well as the rest of us. But with tears already streaming down his face he hoiked himself up over the wall and dropped down, out of sight and scrabbled about on the rough, dirt floor. Long, agonising minutes passed before he reappeared, hands and face smeared with coal dust and grimy tears, holding in one dirty hand a couple of lumps of old, greyish meat.

"Come here, Robert!" the headmistress commanded. He shuffled forward to stand in front of her. "Open your hand and let me see the meat." He did so, gazing down in terror at some ancient mess, well-chewed but not by him. "Put it in your mouth, Robert," she ordered. "Chew hard and swallow and let this be a lesson to you not to throw away any food. You eat what you are given. Do you understand?"

"Yes, Miss," he mumbled. Then, as we watched, horrified, he tried again and again to put the lumps of meat in his mouth, but at the last minute, couldn't. At last he did it and, chewing hard with tears streaming down his face, managed to gulp the meat down.

It was a hard lesson to learn, not only for poor Robert but for all of us. It was cruel and certainly wouldn't be allowed today. But you have to remember it was wartime and things were different then.

Ruth Eavis has happier memories of school days in the '40s:
My memories are of walking up through the churchyard to school. After school dinners we had our rest on little coconut mats we'd pull out to lie down: I remember lying between Brian Whatford and Colin Rose!

I was always very friendly with Margaret Miles, Talbot as she was then. One very clear memory was that we'd been to the shop and we'd only one bicycle between us. We decided that I would stand on the pedals and she would sit on

Pilton School after the war: School photo from 1949
Back Row: *Pat Hill, Molly Dredge, George Higgins, Robert Hurley, Diana Watch, Shirley Dredge, Molly Parsons, Angela Henderson*
Second Row: *Philip Eavis, Graham Atwell, David Down, Edward Trott, Valerie Whatford, Diana Boyce, Dorothy Hughes, Ruth Eavis*
Third Row: *Mrs Grace Connock (Infants), Nancy Atwell, Pat Darch, Michael Ball, Pat Flower, Joy Salisbury, Annette Grant, Michael Loxton, Neville Henderson, Mrs Margaret Turford (Head)*
Fourth Row: *Hedley Lomas, David Snook, James Dredge, Barbara Flower, Brian Hurley, John Curtis, Alan Blacker, Mary Cox*
Front Row: *Patsy Dredge, Doreen Whitcombe, Susan Eavis, Elizabeth Hill, Ann ?, James Govier, Ann Chapman, Graham Watch*
The following attended the 2008 reunion: *Pat Hill, Molly Dredge, Angela Henderson, Philip Eavis, Valerie Whatford, Diana Boyce, Ruth Eavis, Pat Darch, Michael Ball, Joy Salisbury, Neville Henderson, Hedley Lomas, James Dredge, Susan Eavis, Elizabeth Hill, Jim Govier, Ann Chapman*

the seat. Off we went down Shop Lane, only to get to the bottom to find that the brakes had given out. So we went over Sir George Forestier-Walker's wall: to this day I have scars on my knees to prove it, and Margaret does too.

Another memory is walking down the lane to Doughy Hallet the baker in Bakery Lane, going in and this incredible smell of baking bread with the furnace going and Doughy having these huge wooden pallets pressing the bread out, still hot. The smell and the whole thing, him in his whites and flour everywhere, is a very dear memory.

Our childhood memories of Worthy were great. My father, brother of Joe, Michael and Philip's father, was born there. As children, the farm was heaven:

bringing the cows in, I used to do hand-milking, there were loads of little fields with magical names, Henhouse Ground, Wagon Ground and Holts, with meadows of wild flowers where we used to pick handfuls of cowslips and violets.

Strickland's was a treasure trove: everything in cardboard boxes but Audrey Strickland always knew where things were. We used to get *Mint Imperials* and she'd say "In the box over there." Janet Rose, or Vigar then, was a great friend of mine. It was the first time we bought cigarettes: we must have been about 12 and we bought a packet of ten *Craven A* because the slogan was it didn't affect your throat. So we bought this packet, no problem about age in those days. We went straight up into the park at Springfield, sat under a chestnut tree, and smoked them until we felt sick!

Aunt Dorothy had Springfield as a Nursing Home and we stayed there for a while before moving to Burnham in the 1950s.

Michael Eavis remembers a bit further back:
I was five when I went to Pilton School. I wasn't very clever or anything, I was quite sort of timid I suppose, and stammering a bit, I was under the protection of Jasser Perry at school, "Don't you touch Joe." He called me Joe; so they daren't hit me or anything, because Jasser was always watching. He went over to Canada when he was 18 and comes back every year and I still thank him but he says, "Isn't it strange how the tables have turned?"

The great thing was running around picking conkers and having conkers fights at school and trying not to cheat, such as putting conkers in the oven, which some people did so they wouldn't ever break. The best trees were around here in Ashes, we used to rummage around here before and after school. It's called Ashes because of the ashes from the limekiln when they actually built the Tithe Barn and they chucked all the ashes out there.

We had a dairy farm, had to take our turns at milking by hand. We had to milk about six cows at the weekend because the proper farm worker was a Baptist preacher, so he didn't milk on Sundays. He came down with the conscientious objectors during the war. My memory of milking at weekends was a chore we all had to cope with. We went to the Chapel twice on Sundays and usually in the middle of the week as well. Chapel to me was always about singing more than anything else. There was one really good preacher called George Osborne from Shepton who made wooden horse-drawn carts, called putts. They had wooden wheels and I used to see him making the spokes fit the hub of the wheel. He was an incredible preacher and made it work for everyone, real star quality. This is between 1945-50.

My father was a preacher as well, and mother did relief teaching to keep paying the bills. She earned more from that than father did from the cows, I'm sure. She held it all together with her teaching job and she was stern and wanted us all to do well and she was quite strict. She was the main thrust of the family because she was powerful and knew what she wanted. So we had quite a strict upbringing in a way but it eased off later in life.

Early in 1950, Wensley Hunter Bond of Burford passed away. The Bond memorial gates made by village blacksmith, Tom Boyce, can still be seen by the church. Their parallel stories evoke times of an earlier era. Christopher Bond writes of his grandfather, an anonymous writer described Tom Boyce on his retirement in the 1970s:

Wensley Hunter Bond was a barrister and farmer, born in Ireland, and moved to England after Ireland became independent: the house was burnt down by Sinn Fein in 1922. He farmed Old Burford Farm until 1947, seeing the revolution from horse ploughs to tractors. He thought he could raise two crops of beef here each year, but found not as much rain as in Ireland so turned to dairy cattle instead.

He was blind in one eye so gave up being a barrister (too many papers to read). Despite this he was a good shot and started the pheasant shoot at Burford. He had a gamekeeper/woodsman who used a cart-horse to extract tree trunks. He provided meat for the household during the Second World War through shooting pigeons (two shots per flying bird). He was a County Councillor and

Wensley Hunter Bond, (right) together with James Bond

Church Warden, and active in the county. His children remember the weekly ritual after the Sunday roast lunch, of picking up stones from ploughed fields which had mysteriously grown on the surface since the last week.

I was a small child when he died but can remember being driven by him in a horse-drawn cart to Shepton market (very rough on the roads) and collecting groceries from the old-fashioned grocery shop there. When he died I was thought too young to go to his funeral in Pilton but vividly remember running after the funeral cortège going down the drive. The wrought iron gates at the church were given in his memory; a later plaque added my father's and eldest brother Rodney's names.

Wensley's Anglo-Irish wife Amy was 20 years younger and had six children; the eldest, James, inheriting Burford in 1970. She had a strong personality: rode to hounds side-saddle, was a member of the Synod of the Church of England, embroidered copes (made out of her sailing father's gold epaulettes) and hassocks, still in use at Wells Cathedral. She made fine silk landscape pictures which she exhibited in London and created a well known Alpine Garden (opening a quarry in the farm from which stones were brought by horse and cart to the house) which she opened to the public under the National Gardens Scheme.

Mains services came late to Burford: I can remember the family in ever colder circles surrounding the one open fire in her sitting room, going to bed with a saucer and candle and breaking the ice in the basins in the (very few) bathrooms. Her treatment of snails (put them in an acid bowl) also remains a strong memory.

As a child I enjoyed taking a shotgun into the woods to shoot pigeons and squirrels. I used to see/imagine the famous 'Beast of Pilton' behind trees as I came home in the dusk (once I shot an ant hill which I am sure had two ears) and caused uproar by proudly bringing a rook chick into her breakfast room. She often led a group of six or more family walking to church on Sunday. I hated the climb back up the hill to Burford Cross but stories of the phantom coach and horses which drives past Pilton Manor on starry nights – invisible but jingling as it passes – helped to pass the time.

Tom Boyce spent the whole of his life in Pilton and more than anyone else, represents the change from the old village with its long ancestry of craftsmen into the age of mechanisation of modern agriculture.

Tom was born in 1910. His grandfather, also Thomas, had been a farmer but decided to become a blacksmith. He settled in Pilton in 1860 and set up his forge in the yard of the old butcher's shop.

This space had previously been the old village pen, into which the Waywarden used to impound straying horses and cattle whose owners had to pay a fine before they were released. When Thomas Boyce settled in the village, there were three other blacksmiths, one near the old garage, one near Barrow Cottage. Not only did Mr Boyce make shoes for horses but he also made complete ploughs and would take his metal to Shepton Mallet for casting. He became a metal worker and his work can still be seen in the Parish Hall gateway and in ironwork on the bier house door. He became Church Warden when Horace Faithful Grey was vicar. Even as late as 1920 there were still 100 horses in the village

Tom Boyce with church gates in memory of Wensley Hunter Bond, 1959

but gradually as numbers dropped, so the blacksmiths' forges closed until only Tom's father remained.

Tom's earliest memories include horses being led through the village, to be used by the BEF in France in the First World War. As a boy, he attended the village school at Pilton until he was 12. Then he went to Shepton Mallet Grammar School and left aged 16 to become a clerk with the Great Western Railway, but his heart was not on books but on metal and machines. So he left and joined his father on the forge. A frequent visitor in those days was Colonel Garton from Pylle, who collaborated in a scheme for metal work and founded the Somerset Guild of Craftsmen.

Tom himself became a real craftsman, as can be seen in his work in the Church gates erected to Mr Bond of Burford, the three rails on the north side of Wells Cathedral and in many skills in the 'craftsmen's church' at Pylle. Apart from metal work, Tom's heart was in cricket. Every Tuesday and Thursday evening he was bowling in the nets at Shepton Mallet and every Saturday and Sunday after church, he set off on his motor bike for matches. When the Playing Field opened in 1966, Tom became captain of Pilton's first cricket team.

In 1940, Tom joined the RAF serving in a Repair and Salvage Unit. For two years he served in the 8th Army; after he was demobbed he returned to his forge. The War Agricultural Committee was running Steanbow Farm and still using horses, but in 1955 the farm went into private ownership and tractors took the place of horses. The forge was in small demand and Mr Tincknell, knowing Tom's ability, invited him to join the firm and repair agricultural machinery. There he worked until his retirement in 1975.

Thomas & Gilbert Boyce at the Forge 1937

To live in a village, *said Tom,* one must be part of a village; unless you do, you soon lose touch. As I grow older, there are so many new people I just don't know them, but I would never want to live anywhere but Pilton.

The 1950s
CORONATION CELEBRATIONS 1953

Queen Patsy Dredge, with Elizabeth Hill,
Beulah Cook, Roseanne Pearce,
Margaret Payne

Joe and Sheila Eavis as Henry VIII
and one of his wives

Ann Chapman (Millard) and Pauline Parry (Wilson)

1950s Britain was still in recovery after the Second World War, which mercifully left rural Somerset unscathed. Ration cards were still in use to begin with but gradually things improved for all. Pilton, along with the rest of the country, celebrated the Coronation of Queen Elizabeth II in 1953, as told by villagers who were children at the time.

Tony Bailey remembers schooldays in the 1950s and how he heard of the death of Queen Elizabeth's father, King George VI on 6th February 1952:
School meals were cooked in kitchens in Shepton and brought in insulated containers. The older lads used to help bring it in and I can remember the man who delivered it saying, "The King has died." I shall never forget that, I was quite sad. We hadn't been going to Pilton School long but with father killed in the war, we could have had an education at the army's expense. To start with, we went to a convent in Shepton but there was such an influx that they made it girls only, so all the boys got kicked out. So we went to Pilton: we could have gone to the Cathedral School but we'd have to have been boarders as there weren't regular buses.

I remember there used to be a hole in the wall into the Manor gardens where there was a nice pear tree. We used to put our hands up and say "Please, Miss, can I go to the toilet?" which was out round the back. Of course, we'd be out, over the wall, pinching the pears!

Tony started gardening in later life because at Shepton:
I disliked the music teacher. She would never punish a pupil herself, she said to go and see Mr Saxon who used to say "Right, go out and do some gardening." I used to love that. The two gardening masters were brilliant. So we had a good education in gardening, because we had a potting shed where we used to sterilise soil, propagate plants from cuttings, seeds. All from 11 plus. We used to do double digging, dig off 9″ of soil, put it at the back end, then turn over 6″ or 8″ below.

Douglas Turner, in an otherwise highly personal book edited and published by his daughter Shannon following his death in 2003, Five Farms, A Somerset Farmer's Life, *describes when he came to Old Burford Farm in 1947:* "It had never been let before. It was a big farm, 210 acres plus some grass keep, so it was a real step up the farming ladder."

In 1950, following a whirlwind romance, he married an Australian, Gwen, who according to Philip Eavis, was "a truly free spirit with a real sparkle." They began life together at Old Burford: When I originally went to Burford I decided I'd try to set up my own milk round, selling my milk retail. I bought a new A40 van and milk bottling equipment, and bottled Burford milk. I sold it in the village for several years, but gradually people wanted a better quality milk. Unlike today, 'quality' then meant a higher butterfat and so we bought three Guernsey cows, Marazion, Penzance and Redruth. At that time Cornwall was famous for its Guernsey herds, although of course they originated from the Channel Islands, but we called our first cows after Cornish cows because that's where they were strongest. These three became the forerunners of my herd at Perridge.

Forerunners too of his daughter Judith's Brown Cow Organics story. The makings of a future animal lover and vet in son Steve are described:
We lost Stephen on the farm one day when he was just a toddler. Mother and Dad were down for the day from Paulton, and we panicked and went madly looking for him. But we also noticed that Brambles, our Springer Spaniel, was missing. Stephen and Brambles were always together and we were looking everywhere when we found them in a flower bed in the garden, quite a long way for a toddler to walk.

John Fletcher writes of a story told him by Stanley Williams:
In 1952, a colossal downpour hit the West Country. Large parts of Lynton and Lynmouth and many of their inhabitants were tragically swept away to sea. The rain also hit Pilton.

Just as at a recent Festival when a sort of tidal wave swept down the valley swamping everything, a similar phenomenon hit the ford at Cockmill in '52. This was unfortunate for the young driver of the bread van, whose vehicle, while crossing the stream, was unceremoniously picked up and swept off down the valley.

Stanley Williams' painting of Cockmill; the Lynton Lynmouth floods were on 12th August 1952

The youth rushed to the Williams's farm at Cockmill, found Stanley Williams, and begged him to get his tractor to pull him out. Stanley took a look at the situation. "Come on," begged the youth, "I've got customers to serve." But Stanley wasn't budging. He was not only a farmer but also a highly gifted amateur artist. As the youth cajoled him he remarked that he'd never seen anything like this before, collected his easel and paints, set them down on a dry bit of ground by the now capsized bread van, and calmly recorded it all for posterity.

That day no one in Pilton got any bread.

In 1953 plans were laid for celebrating the Coronation in a series of committee meetings not dissimilar to planning the 2012 Jubilee. Pilton Parish Magazine, forerunner of Roundabout, described what eventually happened:

On the Monday evening a United Service, with a large congregation present, was held in the Parish Church and on Coronation Day there was a special Holy Communion at 8am. At 2pm the Carnival assembled for judging; at 2.30pm the procession moved off, led by Mr R. Grant on horseback, followed by Carnival Queen, Patsy Dredge, and her four attendants, Elizabeth Hill, Roseanne Pearce, Beulah Cook and Margaret Payne.

The procession also included Mr J. Toogood and his musicians and Mr A. Connock with loudspeaker van and music. From 2pm to 3pm the church bells rang out in loyal greetings to Her Majesty and at the same time formed a joyous background to the Carnival Procession. Apart from house decorations, the War Memorial was decorated with flowers.

At 4.30pm well over 100 children sat down to their Coronation tea in the Wesley Chapel Schoolroom, kindly lent for the occasion. After tea the children were each presented with a copy of the New Testament.

From 8pm onwards there was a social in the Parish Hall, this included refreshments and a wireless was fixed up so that all who wished could listen to the Queen's broadcast.

On the Saturday afternoon the Children's Sports and Comic Football Match took place on the Fair Field: these had to be postponed on Coronation Day because of the weather. After the Sports a large Coronation cake was cut and handed round.

Tony Bailey remembers: it was all a bit of a Carnival. We used to live with Gran in one of Pilton House cottages but moved up to Culverwell. I remember watching carts go by.

The Carnival had categories for Mounted Entrants, Decorated Pram with Occupant, Decorated Bicycle or Tricycle, Most Comic Entry, Most Original and Best Tableau. A handful of the prizewinners are still in Pilton today.

The Comic Football Match was in drag, restaged in tribute at the 1977 Silver Jubilee.

Cyril Chapman dressed as Old Mother Riley

Coronation football match in drag 1953

Behind left to right: Margaret Windsor, Florrie Flowers, Doreen Cox, Phyllis Higgins, Ada Plumley, Ivy Fleming, Marjorie Carter, Arthur Ball

Front left to right: Megan Roberts, Evie Plumley and Kath Long

Pauline Hobbs (née Rodgers) won First Prize in the Mounted Entrant category and remembers the day thus: I spent most of Coronation Day in front of my grandmother's new television, bought specially for the occasion, in the sitting room of the butcher's shop. I was sitting comfortably right in front of the set when Uncle Ern, the butcher, brought his friends over from the Crown. I had to move to the floor and recall Met Corp's leather gaiters beside me, such a strange piece of footwear, polished to a high shine for the occasion.

Pauline Hobbs on prize-winning pony Flicka, by the butcher's shop

Philip Eavis also recalls his fascination with the new-fangled television:
My memory of the Coronation in 1953 is somewhat mixed. Alfie Connock, the builder and funeral director, had bought a television for the occasion – the first to Pilton – and this exciting new technology (a word never used in the '50s) interested me far more than the Coronation itself. Alfie and my father were great friends so our family was invited in to see this new wonder.

The picture would now be regarded as awful, grainy and disappearing many times throughout the transmission (another new word!). The television was far more significant to me than the Coronation.

The village celebrations were held in the Fair Ground (or Field) behind the Gould complex. It was a most unsuitable field for sports as it was on a slope and, I remember, very rough. Nonetheless this was where all village events had been held over the centuries but I think it was the last time it was ever used. (I may be challenged on this!)

I was 14 at the time and remember taking part in the races but being beaten in the final by Georgie Higgins, who then lived at Cutlers Green but emigrated to Australia.

The teas for the occasion were prepared in the Chapel Schoolroom. I recall Winnie Boyce being there, taking charge of the operation, much to the irritation of my mother. Everyone seemed to be singing "*How much is that doggy in the window*" which was top of the Hit Parade at the time. Whenever I hear that somewhat stupid song I think of Pilton's Coronation celebrations at the Fair Ground.

The Coronation Bench made by Bill Appleby for many years occupied a prime position up at Burford Cross.

Pat & Ruby Fleming sitting on the Coronation Bench, made by Bill Appleby

Carolyn Griffiths describes the many branches of the Fleming family:
In the 1950s my grandparents, Winifred and Walter Fleming and all their children but one lived in Pilton. Most by now were adults with their own families: Doug, Grace (my mother), Harold, Derek, Patrick and Philip. Shirley left the village and continues to live in Shepton Mallet.

Doug and Ivy had two children, Katrina and Braddon, the former still lives in the village with her husband, Brian Hurley. Grace and her husband, Seth Griffiths (my parents) had two children, brother Nicholas and myself. My partner, Mikael Nyblom and I have recently returned to Pilton.

Doug was a signalman at West Pennard railway station and recalls watching the Coronation on TV at the Railway Inn, now the Apple Tree. Pat's wife Ruby recalls him fitting the original Coronation Seat by the Burford crossroads. Pat worked for Colin Rose, before becoming a self-employed builder and decorator, working for many houses in the village. He was a well-known and much-liked character. Like all the Flemings, Pat was particularly fond of the countryside and wildlife around Pilton and was often seen out walking, gathering dandelions for his pet birds.

The Fleming family outside the Village Hall in the 1950s

In 1955, following the death of Joe Eavis aged only 54, eldest son Michael began farming at Worthy Farm:

I wanted the farm to continue: my father died when I was 19, so I had to leave the Merchant Navy and come out of a contract with Union Castle Shipping, which was hard enough. Because of the call-up situation, I went down the mines. In other words, saved the farm from being sold. They wouldn't let me stay home, there was no procedure for not being called up (for National Service) except going down the mines. We got £25 a week which was a fortune in those days, £100 a month after tax. That's what made the farm work. I was milking in the morning, then dayshift down the mines, then milking when I got home.

The farm started picking up because I had the energy to keep it going. Mother took on the overdraft. The other brothers were too young: I was the only one who'd left school, so it was down to me. Patrick became a headmaster, he was always head boy of everything. Philip was a farmer but he transferred his energy into Living Homes, which suited him a lot better. So I've been here ever since.

What subsequently happened to Worthy Farm from the '70s onwards has been very much part of Pilton's recent history.

Only a handful of long-term residents will be aware that a master storyteller lived in Pilton in the 1950s, in the days before his books and resulting films encapsulating the Cold War in Europe and latterly, the evil machinations of multinationals, enjoyed worldwide success. John le Carré was yet to emerge but his creator, David Cornwell, has generously sent his early reminiscences of Pilton:

I came to Pilton in, I think, November of 1954, with my newly acquired bride Ann, in the best Evelyn Waugh tradition. After two years at Oxford, I had suffered irreparable financial damage in the wake of my father's very public bankruptcy. I couldn't pay my battles and didn't seem to qualify for university grants or loans. I came down and, with no prospect of completing my university course, married and took a job as an unqualified assistant schoolmaster at Edgarley Hall in Glastonbury, the preparatory school attached to Millfield School at Street. For £8 a week I taught French, Latin and boxing and occasional German to boys between 8 and 13 who had been – usually wrongly – decreed unfit to keep pace with their schoolfellows. In most cases that just meant lazy parenting, lounging at the back of class and not attending. The remedy, as offered by Edgarley, was small classes and more intensive teaching, but that didn't stop the boys from producing a subversive magazine emblazoned with the motto 'we're here because we're not all there,' to the rage of Millfield's founder and headmaster.

And we lived in Pilton: first, but just for a couple of months, with Farmer Toogood at Cumhill Farm, but Toogood was not a comfortable landlord and we quickly moved into a tiny cottage, one-up and one-down, at the top of the village. I forget the address. There was no sanitation, just an outside 'Elsan' privy that we had to empty at night into a hole that I dug in the garden. For a bath, we had a tin tub and heated the water from a shilling-in-the-slot machine that we rented from the electricity company. £8 a week didn't stretch to bus fares into Glastonbury, so I borrowed a sit-up bicycle from my wife's uncle. When I took the bus, the conductor often forgave me the fare, knowing I was a penniless schoolmaster.

Pilton, like villages the world over, was a-buzz with gossip and scandal. The manor was occupied by Roman Catholics: the Phipps family. No decent Protestant spoke to them. They were very jolly, had numerous daughters and lived in genteel poverty. Colonel Phipps claimed to be the last British officer to take part in a mounted cavalry charge. A Mr Blunt of the village had once been an Anglican priest and converted to Rome. He too must be shunned. Absolute power rested with the Misses Bethell, two maiden aunts, as I understood it, who decided who was acceptable and who was beyond the pale. Needless to say, Ann and I were beyond the pale. A Colonel Forestier-Walker, if I have the name right, took us in his kindness to a local race meeting and, finding the car park full, blamed it on the Jews. Somehow, Ann and I put together a drama club. The 'Pilton Players' presented *Night Must Fall.* I played the evil Danny. Wonderful Teddy Stone made illicit hooch from apples, and brought it at night to our door. Thank you, Teddy. And thank you, most of all, Lincoln College, Oxford, for rescuing me from Millfield and enabling me to finish my degree.

But Pilton was perfect. No writer's life can be complete without a Pilton.

© *David Cornwell, May 2012*

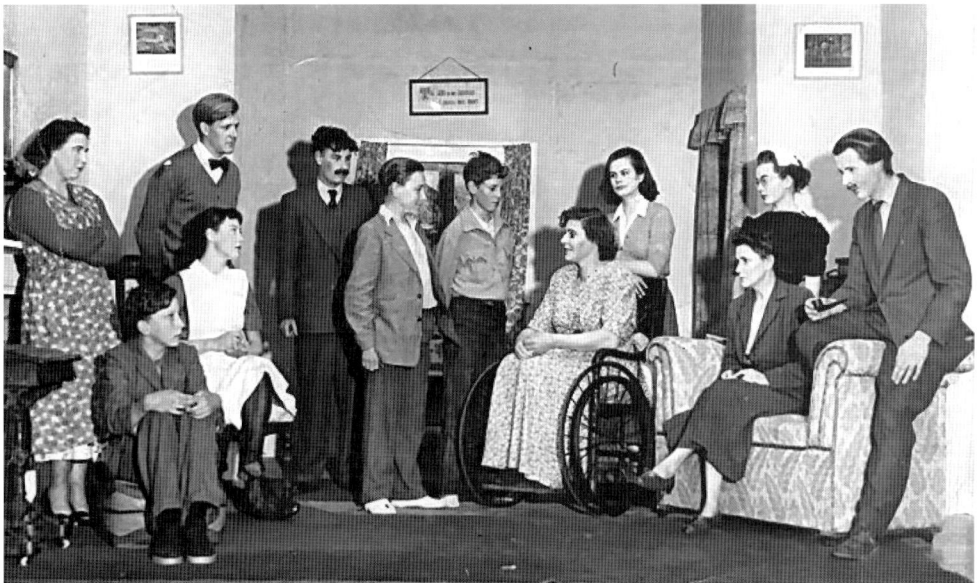

Pilton Players' production of 'Night Must Fall'

David Cornwell graduated with a first-class honours degree in modern languages. He taught at Eton from 1956-58 and was a member of the British Foreign Service from 1959 to 1964, serving first as Second Secretary in the British Embassy in Bonn and subsequently as Political Consul in Hamburg. He started writing novels in 1961, and since then has published 22, several of which became major TV series or award-winning films. He is currently working on a new novel and adapting others for the screen.

An appeal was launched in October 1955 with a minimum target of £409 to send the church bells back to the foundry for repairs. The Crown Inn, then in the hands of Ken and Marj Hardacre, raised £30, mainly by a pole of halfpennies: no less than 4,929 totalling £10-4s-½d weighing 60lbs, plus £5, £1 and 10 shilling notes and the odd cheque.

The church bells returned from the foundry, with Eileen Hiscox as a child

The Tower of Halfpennies collected at the Crown. From left, Fred Harvey, Tom Harris, Eddie Lambert, Ken Hardacre, Rev Hurst Bannister

Liz Elkin describes how in 1952 her family moved next door to Mary and Ron Talbot when they left the cottage on Mount Pleasant for Culverwell, where they enjoyed the new experience of hot water from the copper and an indoor lavatory: Was there a time when Ron Talbot was not a bellringer? He drove coaches for Ted Gould and there is an account in 1954 when, on a ringer's outing, Ron rang in all five towers and drove the bus. He also tended the church clock, keeping it wound and changing the hour in spring and autumn from the 1950s until an electric system was installed.

Ron could fix almost anything and he used his ingenuity and wealth of useful 'bits' to keep the clock ticking; Heath Robinson

Ron Talbot and church clock

would have been impressed. The stone steps in the church tower are worn and Ron was proud that his countless trips had contributed.

Years ago he met someone who had recently moved into the village. "How do 'ee like living in Pilton?" he enquired. They replied that they liked the village but not the weekly bell practice. "Saw the tower on the church before you bought the house did 'ee?" asked the man of the tower as he walked away.

Church bellringers, with handbells visible behind, from L to R Eddie Lambert, Little Bob Harris, Rev Hurst-Bannister, unknown, Ron Talbot and Tom Harris

Liz Elkin describes her mother Margaret Windsor's role in the story of the hand bells still in use today:

Frederick and Albert Harvey donated the hand bells to the Church Tower in 1947 and they were hanging in the ringing chamber in the mid '50s. Margaret Windsor (née Harvey) was appalled to see the state of the hand bells on one trip to the tower so she rescued them. In the damp the leather straps had grown some kind of mould and the metal was tarnished, so she took them home to look after them. They lived in a trunk but were often taken out and hung on a broom handle suspended between two dining chairs, where we tapped out tunes with wooden spoons. Carols and songs were tapped by one and transcribed by another, ready for the team to perform on the Pilton Christmas hand bell circuit when they were rung in all weathers. Although we were careful it is good to see the hand bells are now treasured, each bell has its own bag and the ringers wear gloves. Frederick, Albert and Margaret would be delighted that the hand bells are cared for and that they are still rung by villagers today.

In a decade where Bill Haley and Elvis rocked around the clock and teenagers were invented, along with Teddy Boys and jiving, and urban children played in bomb sites, childhood in a village like Pilton was carefree and mostly car free too, as this collection of memories shows:

We were two or three years old when the Queen came to the throne, the members of our 'gang,' a loose band of half a dozen of us. Not that we hung around together when we were three, except when our parents pushed us out to the Bush for some fresh air and half a pint in the summer. We all enjoyed the same privilege though, growing up in Pilton in the '50s with unimaginable freedom.

We did not all attend Pilton School but we spent our free time together, much of which centred on the stream. We paddled in the ford, lifted stones to look for small, black bloodsuckers and to build the dam, a never-ending task of building and rebuilding pointlessly, as we could not hold back the water and had no real plan to do so. Wellies had to be worn in the stream because the potential bloodsucker attack on bare feet was too terrible to contemplate. The water always poured into the wellies, even when the stream was shallow, so civil engineering projects were always followed by climbing the hollow tree in Barrow Lane, where socks and boots festooned the branches until hunger drove us home. One summer we set ourselves the task of walking in the stream from East Town to Ashes. We started west of Wellands, as we

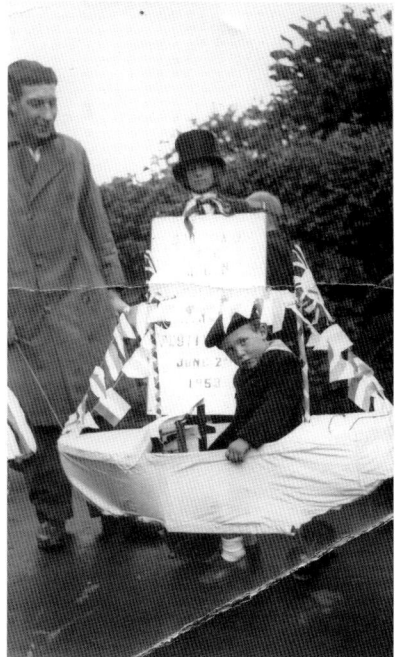

Paul Windsor in home made boat

suspected some householders would not welcome our expedition involving their garden. All went well until we got to Strickland's corner, where the brook disappeared into a tunnel to emerge in Lower Street. We all knew of the bottomless pit in the middle but some adventurous souls managed to navigate round it. Plans of this nature always commenced late in the afternoon, so the final push was the day after, forging a watery path through nettles and brambles, under and over bridges, until we reached the Manor.

Our longer treks often crossed the railway line. Cockmill had a crossing and our excursions to Larcome's Leap sometimes coincided with Mrs Higgins closing the gates. As the train steamed through we were in awe of its size and the noise.

Pennard Hill was covered in bracken and we crawled, commando style, with bracken on our heads, avoiding capture. As we crossed the railway track, we sometimes placed a penny or stones on the line, so we could examine the dust or the size of the penny on the return journey. Once, when we took our parents to the hill, we encountered several rabbits with myxomatosis. Our mothers encouraged us to run on ahead while our dads despatched the poor creatures. We chose not to place items on the line that day, not sure that our parents would understand the scientific significance of our actions.

Knowle Hill was another destination. We scrambled through the gorse and spent hours at Friar's Oven climbing the cliff face and lighting little fires. There was a railway with a steep bank sloping down to the track: only the foolhardy climbed the fence.

Cricket was played in Top Street. We could have used fields but the bounce was poor and it didn't take long to move the bucket if a car should invade the pitch. During one game the ball hit Met Corp's bicycle wheel, he wasn't happy. "If I thought thee's done that on purpose I'd stick this pitchfork through 'ee." He had a fork on the bike so we were more careful in future.

Autumn meant apples, nuts and conkers. The village had several orchards and we knew where to scrump Beauty of Bath, Sheep's Nose and Charles Ross. The best conker trees were at East Town and the champion tree was opposite Chanters. One of our gang had a 99er but never played for 100 because it had the gripes.

Bonfire night was brilliant: Health and Safety had not found Pilton and we were experimental. Hoppers were tied to rockets, bangers tied to rocks and dropped into the stream, bangers tied to rockets – no lasting injuries sustained, we were lucky!

But the best thing, the very best thing, was snow. We had snow every year, definitely, and Pilton is hilly. Mount Pleasant was favourite because it was north facing and the snow lasted. It was rough though and the barbed wire in the hedge at the bottom was a challenge. We were all great on a sledge, feet first, head first, one behind another, two high, face down; we tried them all. The magic years, when the snow froze, we sledged by moonlight in Peace, Barrows and Oathills and we flew.

This idyllic childhood was of its time and place. Pilton was a playground, all of it, every pond, field and tree and we had total freedom to discover it all.

Another of Liz Elkin's childhood memories is of fruit picking:
In the '50s Colonel Whittock lived at The Cedars and he grew blackcurrants on the land within the square enclosed by Barrow Lane, John Beales Hill and Top Street. In summer the blackcurrants all ripened at the same time and several local women were casually employed to pick the ripe fruit. Most women did not work outside the home then and Colonel Whittock was happy for mothers to bring their children with them while they laboured. The children were pretty safe as they played in the sun, although I remember an unfortunate close encounter with ants after sitting on a mound.

Once we were old enough, children were allowed to pick too and we tended to gather with our friends, eat blackcurrants, chat and have fun. We were paid by the basketful, which was weighed in by Mr Dredge. Due to our lackadaisical approach it took a long time to fill a basket and we were paid very little per container. I hit upon a plan: the basket was lined with leaves and a few small stones found their way under the leaves, so I then picked with purpose to cover the evidence. Mr Dredge took the basket, tipped it upside down into the scale pan, removed all the leaves and stones, smiled and paid me for the fruit. Ah well, I was full of blackcurrants for free!

Blackcurrant picking. Ada Plumley standing in background, Blanch Chapman picking and Bet Parry in foreground. Children are Stephen Parry and Robert Vickery

Tony Bailey adds:

With the bubblegum you used to buy in the shop, you used to get a little free wire catapult with a rubber band on. We used to pick these nice fat juicy currants, stand up over the bushes and fire them at all the housewives who used to pick to earn a bit of spare cash. That hits you *splodge!* We got turfed out many a time. We used to love that as lads because after we'd finished picking, we went to a wooden shed where Colonel Whittock's wife used to come out with crusty bread and cheese and cups of tea.

Dave Chapman with his milk van

Well-loved Piltonian, David Chapman, had a milk van:

During the '50s and '60s, Dave Chapman worked as a milkman for Nightingale's Dairy. Dave's milk van was a mobile youth club for several of Pilton's youngsters for a few years. This youth club started earlier than most – dawn sometimes. At weekends and during school holidays, the early risers joined Dave on the round and it was such fun. The kids helped by hopping off and on, delivering pints of milk but mostly they laughed, sang, told jokes and generally took the mickey. Dave always had a terrific sense of humour and ran an orderly, happy team.

There was one occasion that all the regulars wished they had experienced but only Spike Leonard was on board that day. Dave and Spike were driving down the hill into Pylle when a wheel overtook them, raced on down the hill then veered to the left to finish far down in the valley. It took them a few moments to realise the wheel was from the milk van. The van came to a halt without mishap, the wheel was eventually recovered and the tale entertained all who heard it except, apparently, Mr Nightingale.

In a year when the only village shop has sadly closed for ever, it is striking to realise how many shops there were, just over half a century ago. The march of the supermarkets has indeed flattened everything within radius. Liz Elkin continues: There was always the butcher and the bakery but these held no fascination for me as a child. Mrs Rogers sold some bread from Park View, Harry brought it home from Wells after his round, and she would cut it, if required, with a hand-wound bread slicer.

Barkle's in Conduit Square was a grocers with an enormous, dark, hardwood counter. The Barkles wore aprons and everything was weighed and put into bags, even the currants which had to be washed at home and the stalks removed. It smelled of ham and also exotically sweet. I relished every visit.

The Long House was a general store where we sometimes bought sweets on the way to Benleigh, to play in the fields on Pylle Road, but Mum had a 'book' at Barkle's so that was where she shopped. The Garage sold cigarettes, matches and a few sweets as well as paraffin. It was possible, even aged 10, to buy all of the above once Mr Gould was assured it was for your Mum.

Mr Norris had his cobbler's shop in Walnut House which also sold ribbon, cotton, buttons and laces. It had a bell on a spring behind the door and this amazing place smelled of leather and polish. I still love the word 'haberdashery.'

Mr Holbrook had owned the Long House but he 'retired' to Lonbain where he had a tiny shop built. We would knock on the bungalow door and Mr H would appear with his keys to unlock the shop and sell us sweets.

To my eyes the most wonderful shop of all was Mrs Strickland's. Push down the latch, the bell would ring and we'd step down into 'Strickies' to be greeted by the smell of cheese, always cut by a wire, and butter which was shaped with pats before being wrapped in greaseproof paper. Some people did their weekly shop there and Mr Strickland would deliver on Saturday evening in his Morris.

The library was behind the door, there was a charge but Gran would stagger home with about a dozen books, only to send me back with some a few days later saying "Can't read these, they'm American rubbish." As kids, our main reason for visiting Strickies would be to collect rations before an excursion, perhaps snowdropping at Cockmill. At the end of the counter was a glass case which held *Mars bars* and *Five Boys* chocolate but sometimes we'd lash out on 2oz of sweets from a jar and *Eiffel Tower* lemonade crystals. A sherbet fountain was a choking joy but the thrilling experience of shopping at Strickies has lasted a lifetime.

Totty Milne remembers: There were several farms within the village and Mr Strickland's, opposite us, had a variety of animals, pigs, cows and chickens and I much enjoyed helping with milking, haymaking and feeding the pigs. The shop rang a very loud bell when the door opened.

Strickland's farm and shop, unchanged even though this photo dates from the 1970s

Pauline Hobbs (née Rodgers) also remembers shops and services:
The butcher's shop was my second home, because both mum and dad helped out when needed, preparing and delivering meat and serving in the shop.

Pilton was able to provide most of the residents' needs and also for the nearby hamlets. The Post Office was in the General Stores, providing a range of services including daily and weekly papers. Customers would phone or drop in their orders and goods were delivered over quite a distance, several times a week.

Strickland's was effectively a corner shop providing for Top Street and East Town; Holbrook's did the same for Bread Street. Cobbler Norris (now Walnut House) as well as mending shoes also provided odds and ends, including sweets and soft drinks. Hallet's bakery (now Burnside) baked daily as well as making delicious fancies. The winding of cream horns fascinated me, as did the enormous mixer with the oddly rotating dough hook. I loved collecting bread warm from the oven and could never resist a nibble as I carried it home across Barrows.

Fishy Marsh delivered each week from Shepton. He stopped his van on the main road, rang a bell and yelled out "fish oh" to hasten customers not already waiting.

The Doctor held a weekly surgery in the front room of Yew Tree Cottage. Our health was also cared for by Nurse Thomas, who lived opposite the War Memorial; she washed and dressed minor injuries and kept an eye on babies and the elderly. Goulds Garage sold petrol and repaired cars. They also ran coaches to provide outings and daily services for schools, shoppers and workers. The conductress on our school bus also washed and laid out dead bodies before burial, and I went through difficult contortions to avoid touching her hands when exchanging fares and tickets, because of her contact with the dead.

Billy Appleby had a carpentry workshop in the old Malt House where he made coffins, which were stacked against the wall, surrounded by the wheels and partly finished furniture he was working on, all covered in dust and sweet-smelling curls of wood shavings. He never seemed to sweep up or have any concerns about the fire risk.

Alfie Connock, left and Charlie Pearce making a coffin at Trevelyan, Whitstone Hill

Alfie Connock was an undertaker who worked from the village, so it seemed as if residents were literally catered for from cradle to grave.

Leisure was well provided for, with Youth Clubs in the Village Hall and Methodist Schoolroom. Adults had the WI, Mother's Union and Working Men's Club and Pub, with skittles and darts always available. Occasional dances were held with music by the Clem White Trio or we danced to records.

One annual highlight was the fete, then held in mid-August, alternating between the Manor and Pilton House, a much more modest affair in those days but still an excuse to wear our best clothes.

Harvest Festival and Supper were opportunities for celebration: the church always looked stunning with a beautiful sheaf of corn fashioned from bread as centrepiece of the display.

The village was a wonderful place in which to grow up, mainly because of the freedom it allowed. We roamed quite freely, until hunger or bad weather sent us home. There seemed to be a collective sense of responsibility around us, keeping us safe, secure and in line with parental expectations.

The shop on the corner of Conduit Square was the Post Office Stores in the 1950s, better known simply as Barkle's. John Barkle writes:
I came to Pilton in October 1950 to work with my parents in the Post Office Stores. My father and his brother were in partnership in Ditcheat Post Office Stores and ran such a flourishing business that it was decided to purchase another local business and continue the partnership.

I was 16 and had always helped in the business and knew how our old-fashioned stores were run. We sent a leaflet to all houses in the village and all the surrounding area (including North Wootton) with the daily papers, stating that we would be offering a complete delivery service for groceries, with weekly or monthly credit facilities, and we would welcome registration for goods that were still on ration. We had newspapers to sort at 6.30am, closely followed by the postmen from Shepton Mallet who delivered the bulk mail to our office and Percy Guppy sorted the letters, then delivered them around the village.

Our store had lovely oak counters and shelving and for the first ten days, after closing the doors at 6pm we were busy scrubbing, painting and filling up the shop with goods late into the evening. This took its toll on my Dad who collapsed with pneumonia and pleurisy, was taken to Bath hospital for several weeks, and he took months to regain full health.

Suddenly I had to know how to run a business very quickly. I learned one of the best lessons in those first few weeks when a smart commercial traveller from *Phul-Nana,* a firm that made toiletries and cosmetics, came in with a case full of samples. We did not stock these products but the presentation was excellent. I ordered bath cubes, talcum powder, bubble bath, toilet water and Eau de Cologne.

Then we ordered face cream and powder, and even lipstick. Finally I ordered *Phul-Nana* perfume, small bottles in a pretty gift box that sold for about 2/6d. As it was near Christmas I thought this would be a good seller in the next few weeks. All the bathroom products sold very well, but I bought too much stock of the perfumed products. When I left Pilton in 1977, even after two complete shop refits, in some of the drawers were saucepan mending kits, lisle stockings, suspenders, embroidery silks and a number of bottles of perfume. What an unromantic lot the men of Pilton were in the '50s!

I also over bought from a famous biscuit manufacturer. One day our normal 'rep' came in with his sales manager, who proceeded to take advantage of my inexperience and sold me almost three times the biscuits that I needed for the month. From these two firms I learned that if unsure of new products, give just a small order and see how quickly the stock sells. You can always ring up and get more stock in.

In those days we bought from as many as 200 manufacturers. I have invoices from most of them in 1950. We also bought stock from local wholesalers. Many items were delivered to our shops by the railway system. Each day Jim Linsley would deliver all the ordered goods that came via West Pennard station. His wife Olive worked for us part-time, as did Mildred Henderson. My mother also worked early sorting papers, during the day and late into the evening doing the book-keeping, and she was happy to let me do all the buying.

Another memorable day was the day all the cast-iron guttering fell down onto the pavement in front of the shop. Luckily it happened just after we shut for lunch, and no person was involved. It sounded as if there had been a road crash on the corner. A building investigation found that the weight of the slated pitch roof was causing the front and rear walls of the building to 'bulge', and also that the roof timbers were full of woodworm. Drastic action was needed and we had a Wells building firm to make the repairs. The whole building was covered in scaffolding, with tarpaulin sheets covering the roof. For ten weeks workmen came and disappeared up into the roof area, taking down the old roof, beams, chimneys etc and replacing with a new flat roof. The foreman asked me to go onto the roof one day to look at a brick chimney from the dining room that was situated at the rear. It had been built so high to give it enough draught that it was actually swaying slightly in the wind now the roof had been removed. He thought he had had too much beer the night before! Rebuilding was a very costly operation, roughly costing the same price as building a new house at that time.

In the late 1950s we had a major refit of the shop. Elizabeth and I went to a shop equipment exhibition at Earl's Court and came back with bags full of leaflets showing what could be achieved in a modernised shop. My father was very supportive of my suggestion that we needed to update the store and turn our counter service into self-service. My uncle at Ditcheat was not convinced but father went ahead and the big weekend arrived.

We closed at noon on the Saturday and an army of tradesmen arrived. All the old oak counters and shelves were ripped out until the shop was empty. The walls were clad with plasterboards and painted. The ceiling was lowered by 18″ and the floor was re-laid. Electricians were putting in new lighting and power points for new fridges. New metal shelving was being installed whilst all this work was going on, continuing all through Saturday and Sunday night and by 8am on Monday morning we had the refit more or less completed.

It had been a marathon weekend. We started to get the shop filled with goods, so that by 2pm we re-opened as a self-service store. It took some of our older customers some time to get used to shopping with a basket and to actually walk around the store and take goods off shelves. We still had a provision and Post Office counter to serve over, and a checkout for the till. When my uncle came over and saw what we had achieved, he realised how much easier the store was to operate and he had a refit at his store within six weeks. So I helped him to refit his shop over another weekend.

Ruth Eavis married Michael in 1958 and moved to Worthy. A year later, in 1959, her sister Margaret married James Cellan Jones, director of prestigious plays and series for TV at a time of creative innovation in the '60s and '70s, and Head of Drama at the BBC from 1976-9. The social revolution was yet to happen at a time when the Church of England remained intransigent about wedding banns. The vicar, Rev Walker, disapproved of 'a mixed marriage,' whether between Methodist and Anglican, or Welsh and English, we shall never know.

Maggie and I both wanted to get married in Pilton Church. Neither of us was a Piltonian although Maggie had spent a lot of her youth at Worthy Farm. We came across a difficulty. We were both working until the night before the wedding. I was living in theatrical digs in Cardiff and Maggie was working in London. So the vicar refused to marry us since neither of us was resident in the village. This was rather difficult. We couldn't change the date, April 2nd 1959, so we had to get an Archbishop's Special Licence and go and swear all sorts of things at the Sanctuary in Westminster. Despite everything, we were married here in Pilton.

As with many others who love the village, when timing and circumstances were right, they returned. 40 years later their son Simon married in Pilton church; in 2013 his daughter, their grandaughter, will be the third generation to do so.

The 1960s

*Ray Norman driving and
Charlie Pearce in foreground*

The Tithe Barn fire 1963

*Marj Hardacre and Chick Leonard
outside the Crown*

*Josie Hiscox with
Tango riding pillion*

1960s Britain was a time of great social upheaval and global change: the Kennedy assassinations, French student riots, Swinging London, The Beatles, the first moon landings and that "giant leap for mankind."

Yet in Pilton, the major events of the '60s were naturally caused: snow for months on end and the lightning strike that so tragically destroyed the thatched roof of the medieval Tithe Barn.

In 1960 there was another disastrous fire, this time intentional. Some agricultural machinery, an old threshing machine, was sold by Chris Strickland and the purchasers only wanted it as scrap, so they deliberately set fire to it in Oathills. Apparently Chris was furious. Totty Milne photographed the scene and remembers how "a large number of folk of all ages turned out for the spectacle."

Machine fire at Oathills

Chris Strickland with Kathleen Milne

Chris Strickland the elder and young Christopher Strickland, also later known as Chris

Totty also remembers how the traffic in the village was less and I used to go along the main road, on my tricycle, to the Old Vicarage, to play with the Walker children. *Imagine trying that on the A361 today!*

John Barkle continues the Barkle's story:
My Dad died in 1961 and Uncle had a stroke just one month later. This was a very difficult time as my uncle never fully recovered. I spent part of each day in both shops and soon realised that you cannot be in two places at once! Things settled into a routine and then came the worst winter storms for many decades in 1962/3. When the weather is bad there is a tremendous community spirit in villages. The snow and ice made the roads impassable. People were helping to dig their neighbours out and were shopping for each other.

One evening at about 7pm when we were cleaning up the shop there was a knocking on the shop window. Owen Boyce, who farmed at West Compton, had made a rough sledge and had struggled over the hills to get supplies for his elderly neighbours. The drifts of snow over the top of Burford were six or seven feet deep. How did he manage to get to our shop and back home again, loaded up with bags of shopping? He had sacking over his shoulders and was freezing. He took as much as he could carry – what a great character!

Michael Eavis and Douglas Turner brought us churns of milk by tractors and we sold milk into jugs with a pint measure. Mr Stevens the baker kept us supplied with bread. We had an almost full tank of paraffin when the snow came which was good for many people who used that fuel for cooking and heating. We were soon running out of stock and the wholesalers could not get out to deliver. I had a large van and drove to one of our wholesalers in Bridgwater with chains on the wheels of the van. I kept on buying sides of bacon, gammons, cheeses and the whole range of food items, as well as salt, (a very important commodity when we have snow), and loading until we could not get any more goods into the van. Luckily I managed to keep the van on the road coming home. As the newspapers came late day after day we were out for hours trying to get them delivered. Three ladies who delivered for us in Pilton were Ella Blacker, Madge Carter and Florrie Flower. They always came up trumps. As

John Barkle with Marylin Pearce and daughter Shelly

we delivered papers and groceries to West and East Compton, North Wootton, Redlake, into part of West Pennard and Sticklynch, our van took a battering and we had many minor 'skirmishes' with other vehicles.

We had a number of phone calls from people all over the area who had seen our van out and about, asking if we could deliver to them, as they could not get their cars out of their drives.

We hoped that some of them would appreciate our service and stay with us as regular customers. Our times in Pilton really were *The Good Old Days*.

Ruth Eavis remembers that hard snowy winter:
In 1962, on Boxing Day, after we'd had a whole lot of friends staying. I went upstairs and looked out of the bathroom window at Worthy and the snow was falling horizontally. That was the last thing we saw for three weeks. We were cut off. The first visit we had was from Auntie Alice, who came walking along the hedges in order to see us. It was compacted snow. Rebecca had been born in November, so we didn't get out at all for three weeks.

Tony Bailey had the snow to thank for his first car:

There'd been some function at the Club. I was walking back home with Norma Vickery who lived up the road from us. On Boxing Day the snow started: you had a job to walk into it, it was blowing from the east and we were walking west to east to go home. You almost had to turn your back on it. Next day there were drifts 6 to 8 feet deep. The roads were unbelievable.

Alfie Connock used to have his coffin workshop on the main road. They had several bodies in the Chapel of Rest in West Shepton. The only way he could get the coffins there was disassembled in planks, on a sledge. A whole gang of us pulled these sledges because there were narrow gaps through the snowdrifts, all the way into Shepton, so they could make up coffins there. We pulled about eight of them.

I went on the Council from late December to the end of March helping clear the snow. I earned enough money to buy my first car.

Liz Elkin remembers the snow as a teenager:

The snow froze every night and there was no let-up, so we didn't go back to school for weeks! Concerns about food and fuel were not for us. Our fathers having to walk to Steanbow to get lifts to work was not our problem. We enjoyed our Scandinavian landscape and we learned some tricks. Falling off your sledge or tray didn't stop the fun, the slide continued on the front of your coat. It was preferable to start to brake well before the stream, as ice is never as thick as it looks.

Drifts up at Burford crossroads

Eileen Taylor (then Hiscox) and cousin David Thomas, son of Gavin and Kathleen (née Hiscox) at 'Piccadilly Circus' on the main A361, by Springfield crossroads

The big freeze was also remembered by Sandra Howe, who had just moved to the village:

It was almost a white Christmas but not quite! The snow, feet of it, fell on Boxing Day – the 26th and then through December 27th 1962. Nobody had told the weather gods about Global Warming: the snow was deeper than in 1947 when I remember it being well over the top of my Wellington boots!

Would we get out round the corner by the church? After further heavy snow over the New Year we couldn't get out of the village, let alone up the hill. We were cut off completely for nearly a week. Never mind, we thought, we can always get everyday supplies from the shop. What we didn't realize was that stocktaking was in full swing and John Barkle had cut down his supplies to a minimum to make it easier for the two stock takers to make their assessment. They were snowed in too and had to find accommodation in the shop. Nor did we ever imagine that temperatures would not rise above freezing once until March 6th 1963. Brr!

Getting to work at school in Bruton was hazardous to say the least but we made it every day bar one, when a Ford Cortina slid in a straight line into our side valve Morris and pushed the radiator against the fan. To get to Bruton we had to go via Shepton Mallet, as the East Compton road – very narrow then – was completely blocked. We could not use Prestleigh Hill for three weeks as the snowdrifts were 15 feet deep across the road. The snow was detonated every day but it blew in again off the fields overnight. The ten miles to Bruton took us two and a half hours in the morning and the same amount of time returning in the evening. Five hours in a car mainly in the dark and with minimal heating. Brr!

Stone Cottage was cold – no central heating and a coal fire in one room which could only be lit on our return from work in the evening. We had no hot water for three months and no water at all for six weeks. Thank heavens for Frank Hiscox who every day, without fail, delivered a milk churn full of water to our front door and for Josie who, for weeks, dried all my washing in front of her kitchen range.

Three months and no bins collected! We flattened cans and burnt as much as we could but the garden was still piled high by the time the lorries eventually reached us.

The bonus was the many, many birds that came down to the snow-covered lawn desperate for any scattered crumbs. I think my bird watching started then.

After the long journey home from work the Crown proved very much more inviting than a cold and frozen cottage. We were warmly welcomed to a roaring fire in the bar and Marj Hardacre provided us with hot soup and sandwiches most evenings. How we blessed her! Eventually we *had* to face driving down the hill and home. With no exaggeration the ice on the *inside* of the bedroom window was an inch thick! We didn't undress to go to bed – we put on more layers and were still cold. Brr! Our kitten, Fred, helped by curling up on the bed beside us. Frank and Josie were very kind to us, so John helped Frank with the cows. Hay was taken out to the fields on the tractor. The snow was so deep that they had to walk along the top of the hedges in order to throw the hay into the fields. This worked well until they reached a gateway invisible under the snow. One step and they were up to their armpits in the white stuff and thankful the gate was not closed! It was amazing how a shared flask of whisky helped to ease the situation!

Animals have a strong desire to survive. Three weeks after the first snowfall a flock of sheep at East Compton were found alive and well and completely buried in snowdrifts at the side of the field. A Mini abandoned on the East Compton Road also survived: it was dug out three months later.

The winter of 1962-63, fifty years ago now, was our first winter in Pilton. We appreciated the community spirit in the village and the never ending help we were given. As a result we made some lasting friends and are still in the village half a century later!

Frank Hiscox by Tom Boyce's ironwork for the Village Hall

John Barkle's 'good old days' were not so good for near neighbours in Conduit Square, as a less natural disaster befell the Rodgers family, who had the misfortune of waking to find a lorry, driven by one Mr Cleverley, not so cleverly driven straight into Durston Cottage. Pauline Hobbs (Rodgers) relates:

In the early hours of May 21st 1962, my grandmother, Frances Rodgers, had a very rude awakening, when her bedroom was nearly demolished by a lorry, delivering concrete girders and crockery to Butlins at Minehead. The lorry driver for a firm from Frome was ironically called Mr Cleverley. He is reported to have said that his brakes failed coming down Whitstone Hill and that he had hoped to have negotiated the village safely, before rolling to a halt at the foot of Park Hill. He hadn't reckoned on the bend, even though he said he knew the road!

Lorry disaster at Durston Cottage

My grandmother had only moved to the cottage days earlier, from the butcher's shop across the road. After the accident, she said that she would return to her house when repairs were completed but that she would probably sleep at the back. In fact, she returned to the same room with hardly a second thought. Surprisingly, people living at the shop and pub did not hear the impact.

I was only 18 and at college in Bristol at the time: the first I heard of the accident was when the College Bursar called at my digs in person, before breakfast, to tell me about the crash before I heard about it in the news and to reassure me that no one had been hurt.

Family who had been living in the cottage were unable to return for a long while, so they moved into Hill Rise on Shop Lane with my mother, while lengthy repairs were carried out. Rather than share my bedroom at home with my grandmother for eight weeks, I decided to take a summer holiday job at Butlins Holiday Camp at Minehead, which is where I met Alan. We have been together for 50 years now: that accident certainly had some long-term consequences!

The storm that hit the medieval Tithe Barn on 22nd June 1963 is still an emotive subject today for anyone who saw it happen. Ruth Eavis recalls:

Rebecca's christening was set for a Sunday in late June 1963. After the service we all went back to the farm and were having christening tea. It was a lovely day but suddenly got incredibly dark and started to pour with rain. Then there was this terrific thunderstorm. The lightning we could see had struck the Tithe Barn. We left various people to look after the children and ran up to the Barn with Jimmy who had a camera.

Within minutes all the timbers were just falling and there was this horrendous fire. The thatch had caught alight.

There's a photograph of me by Gavin Thomas, walking away with the burning Barn behind me. So sad, because from school we used to go into the Barn, we used to watch sheep shearing. It's deeply linked to my memories.

A distressed Ruth can be seen walking away in Gavin Thomas' photo

Tony Bailey was on the way back to the village during the storm:

We'd been to Street that Sunday afternoon, to a café where all the teenagers used to go. There was a terrible thunderstorm, torrential rain and the thunder and lightning were unbelievable. Coming down the straight road by where West Pennard Station used to be, we seen the lightning strike the Barn, seen the smoke start to rise.

By the time we got up to the top of the hill to the Barn itself, the whole of the roof was one mass of flame. The thatch, I guess, and it was starting to fall off.

Luckily I had that little Kodak Brownie camera in the car. It was Neville's car, Neville Henderson, my best man when we got married.

We stayed there until they got it under control. That was an experience. Some of the old boys used to say there was never a nail in that roof but there were hundreds of thousands on the floor when it had all burned off. But they were hand-made blacksmiths' nails, not the ones you get at the DIY now. The main framework would have been pegs.

The lightning struck on the west end. I can remember the finial down on the floor. It was down there for years but then it disappeared.

Tony remembers: when I was a child the fields around the Barn were full of sheep, then the Barn full of sheep being sheared and popping out shorn the other side.

Bob Hiscox, Frank's father said after the fire it was "like an old friend gone" according to Philip Eavis.

Michael Eavis tried to salvage his tractor, stored in the Barn, but the Toogoods, to whom he had lent it, had already salvaged it, as he recalls:
The tractors were all in the Barn, so I rushed back to try and get them out. Jim Toogood had my tractor out already, away from the fire but left his own in there. It burned so fast. Frightening. There's a lightning conductor now. Lightning does seem to strike a lot around here, as we had a strike while the new house was being built. It's very vulnerable: imagine a second strike so close to the Barn within 50 years. That wouldn't burn now because there's no thatch, but even so, it would cause a lot of damage.

The medieval Abbey of Glastonbury not only had their Tithe Barn here, but the Manor was the Abbot's summer home. The Manor House grounds have yielded some interesting archaeological finds as proof of earlier settlements in Pilton. In this photo the Rev John Walker, together with Lady Sarah Baring (then wife of Tommy Baring) who lived at the Manor, looks at tiles and a pot found on the site of the original medieval vineyard. Chris Walker, Tim's elder brother, is in the foreground.

Tim Walker, now a partner in Park Medical Partnership in Shepton Mallet, remembers going around carol singing with about 20 people in December, with himself on trumpet and Chris on flute, being invited in to people's homes, including Smith's bakery, for mulled wine and mince pies. He also remembers:

Christmas service in the church during the '60s and '70s always had Sylvia Butt, who had a very good voice, singing the first solo verse of *Once in Royal David's City.*

In 1964, Nigel and Anne Godden bought the Manor and replanted the land with vines in 1966 and 1968, aiming to expand to 15 acres by 1976/77 so their story continues in the next chapter.

Liz Elkin remembers what it was like to be a '60s teenager:
Would we have enjoyed the '60s even more, we baby boomers, if we had known we were the Golden Generation? More health and wealth than ever before and the *music!* How our children envy us as their retirement shuffles further and further away from them.

Being a teenager in Pilton meant that we were protected from the excesses the '60s had to offer. Glastonbury dances at the Town Hall were epic; every Saturday the crowd equalled the maximum fire regulation figure, exactly, and the bands were local, national and international names. But the last bus through Pilton left at 9pm which necessitated forward planning, so should we:

a) Leave at 8.55pm
b) Make sure a friend was driving our way
c) Thumb a lift
d) Walk all the way, mostly barefoot due to unfortunate footwear

We always plumped for c) which occasionally led to d) but we felt it was worth it for how were we to know that incredible music, in the village, was just around the corner?

Our local cinema was the Regal in Shepton. Again public transport was less than accommodating, many a finale was missed as we left the pictures and ran for the last bus from the top of town.

We spent our evenings hanging around. We rearranged bales in barns like furniture, sat in the bus shelter or on Burford seat and talked, except on Youth Club night. Once a week the usual crowd dressed up, made an effort and looked more attractive, just for the one evening. We played table tennis, put on plays, sang carols at Christmas and played records in the village hall. Then we were offered the cellar under the Working Men's Club, it just needed digging out! And it was. Several teenagers put many hours into clearing it to have a place of their own. It was so cool and, even better, the fire escape was a trap door in the ceiling.

Teenagers in Pilton in the '60s were like teenagers here now, good kids who loved growing up in a wonderful place, until they needed to get somewhere. Times have changed, there is no cinema in Shepton and the last bus back from Glastonbury is at 6.03pm but world-class music has come to Pilton with no bus fare required and free entry, magic!

Women's Tug-o'-War 1962. From right to left: Kath Long, Norma Vickery, Roseanne Pearce (hidden), Hilda Leonard, Margaret Vickery (hidden), Marylin Pearce, Mary Talbot, Phyllis Higgins

Tony Bailey continues:

In the evenings, holidays, weekends, and when I left school, I was working for Philip Eavis on his farm, although I used to help Michael a bit, with hayricks and hedging.

In about '64 they brought the mains drainage to the village and I helped out, working a heavy huge iron 'jackhammer' or pneumatic drill. There were two gangs, one went up the Pylle Road and at one stage I was with the other, near the old Bakery. It was raining, so we were only paid half pay if we didn't work. The other gang was still working, which was resented. The gangs started fighting, hitting each other with shovels, so I thought I'm getting out of here and went home!

When we got married in 1966, at first we stayed in a caravan down at Worthy. I think we were probably the first to do that on site. Rob (Chick) Leonard and I helped them move to the farmhouse and Mrs Perry moved into the cottage before she moved away. Rob used to work for Michael and then I think worked for the artificial insemination service. We were the best of pals. Philip had a pick-up – yes, Chick in the back and Jack Cox on the side of that photo. He was a character and had a brother Tom who dropped a milk churn on his toe which went septic and he lost one of his legs. He used to go to Bridgwater and Tor Fairs and I used to have hazelnuts from Philip, picked them all up and he'd sell them. Jack

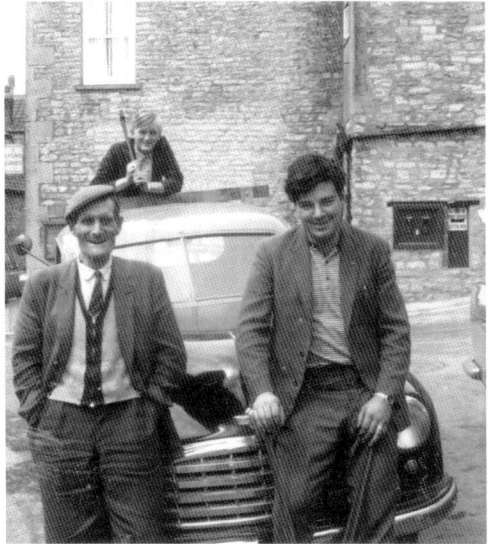

Tony Bailey outside the Crown with Chick Leonard behind and Jack Cox on left

was more of a scrap metal merchant. He used to have little vans or large pick-up lorries and go round getting old scrap from the farmers. A real wheeler-dealer. They were the last people who lived in Leys Cottage before it was done up. It was pretty barren in those days.

1965 was the first year we picked strawberries. I thought it was an easy game but I didn't realise how much work there was! I hired a Rotavator, rotavated those two acres that had been allotments behind Culverwell Cottages, initially planting only half an acre.

We were only at Worthy for six months from March to August. Then I got a job at Perridge for the Calmann's. The head gardener was Mr Snow, a bit like the old Victorian gardeners you see on TV. So it was a good education as well. When Michael had his first Festival we were at Perridge.

Pilton became home for the Cannock family from January 1966. Daphne recalls:
We arrived at Longacre in the snow. We had purchased our field and building plot from Trevor Toogood who was preparing to leave Cumhill Farm. While we built our home around us, we were delighted that the Long House shop on the corner was such an excellent grocery, and Mr and Mrs Taylor such supportive neighbours. Mr and Mrs Bowes who lived at Hyde House, opposite us, took such an enthusiastic interest in our building project that on one occasion Dr Buckler came and ordered Mrs Bowes down from our roof.

Fred Mitchell delivered meat and Eve delivered bread three times a week. We were delighted to have post collected from the box outside our gate. This was marvellously convenient for John's work communications. Mr Henderson was the most helpful postman, and Mr Robinson the most helpful planning officer, so we were surrounded by help.

Our lovely friend Ruth Eavis went to a lot of trouble to help us enjoy becoming part of village life, as did many other kind and supportive friends. We saw the Playschool at the Methodist Church come into being, and I was soon teaching part time in the village school. The Headmistress, Miss Newbon, lived in the school house. Mary Gait taught the infants. Mr Humphries and myself taught the older pupils. Mrs Cashen was the school secretary. The vicar, Rev Walker, very kindly gave half his garden for the children's play area to be extended. After-school activities, such as modern educational dance, were enjoyed by many pupils. I can still picture many of you dancing and engaging in dance dramas, absorbed and delightful.

Not to be left out, the ladies wanted Keep Fit classes. As long as the school was open, we met in the school hall. A room full of ladies exercised to music. Ruth organised the music, I taught the movement, and many will remember the experience. Lovely ladies like Cynthia Mitchell and Grace Griffiths, no longer with us, are bright in our reflections of these shared experiences, to say nothing of many who are still here to chuckle at the memory.

Sadly, the school was sold to the head of adult education for this area, who turned it into his home, and our class had to move. John was persuaded to leave the sitting room at Longacre empty, except for a very comfortable carpet, and Keep Fit resumed at our house! This went on for quite a long time. It was fun, and we were fit!

The school children were all going to West Pennard School, so we no longer heard the lovely sound of play at break and lunch times. Wednesday mornings, mums with pre-school children met at Longacre, and, becoming aware of this, Rev Walker was quick to get us to start a pram service in the church. I think it started a project of weekday pram services across the West Country for a long season. Eventually the Long House shop closed, as did the butcher's and the bakery. Mr Henderson retired, and the village entered a new season. Miss Bethell and Brigadier Bethell from Pilton House had opened their home for the Flower Show for the last time. Miss Tilly still kept her pony events going, but times had changed.

I have wonderful memories of acting in Miss Wilson's drama group, and listening to Margaret Windsor's recitations, as well as picturing many of you, as children, rehearsing for the last school nativity play that took place in Pilton School. The programme for that nativity play is still in the Pilton archive collection.

Daphne Cannock (in uniform)

Carolyn Griffffiths was one of the last to complete her education at Pilton School:
In 1969 the village school closed. I was a member of the last age group to complete my primary education there. We had two teachers and two classrooms for around 60 children aged between 4 and 12. Those two teachers taught all subjects except Religious Education, taught by Rev Walker on Thursday mornings, when all children were distracted by the prospect of swimming lessons in Shepton Mallet pool. Other teachers were Miss Hanson, Mrs Gait, Mr Humphries and Miss Geoffrey and Miss Newbon.

Entertainment outside school included dancing classes, Brownies, the church choir for both children and adults, enthusiastically led by the vicar and accompanied by David England on the organ. Happy memories of Friday evening practices, Sunday services and carol singing. Growing up in Pilton in the '60s made for a wonderful childhood.

Pilton School in the 1960s

Carolyn's Fleming family members were instrumental to the story of Pilton Football Club:
Walter Fleming, my grandfather, founded the original village football team and during the '60s continued to play a part in managing the team and ran the line.

I believe at one time all my uncles played for the team, as did my father until he was 42, after which he ran the line and was Treasurer. The home pitch was Stoney Field which was on a gradient, such there was an advantage to play downhill in the second half! The footballers used the butcher's garage, complete with one tin bath to wash after the game. In later years my brother and all my male cousins, except Gary who lived in Shepton, also played for Pilton FC.

Walter Fleming with British Legion Standard

Walter was a longstanding member of the British Legion and also standard bearer. He took on board responsibility for maintaining the cenotaph. He and Pat were mainstay helpers at the annual Pilton Day, which in the '60s was held at Pilton House.

The Fleming uncles at Steanbow

My grandfather and various uncles used to assist my great uncle Ron Ward press cider at Steanbow.

John Howe encapsulates some characters of yesteryear:

Is it my fond imagination or were there really more memorable characters in Pilton in the old days? Today, we just seem to have to make do with Ray Loxton – rough shooter, jobbing builder and television pundit on all things Piltonian.

When Sandra and I arrived at Stone Cottage in 1962 the first villager we met was Chris Hiscox. He looked over the wall as we unpacked and said "Welcome to Pilton – mind you, you'll have paid too much for that house." He and Jean proved to be great neighbours and a mine of information for us incomers.

Every morning we were woken by Chris's brother, Frank, driving his tractor out to his stall at Cockmill with his faithful collie alongside. (This pattern of farmhouse in the village and fields towards the edge of the parish was a relic from Saxon times). Josie Hiscox followed on foot when her chores were done, to help with the milking and mucking out. A year later I sold her my old moped and she became a village celebrity making the journey every day with the collie dog proudly riding pillion.

In those days the village verges and drains were kept immaculately by Fred Gadd and Mr. Fleming. We never locked

Josie Hiscox on her motorbike, with Tango who went everywhere with her

our door when going to the shop because we knew they kept an eagle eye on everything going on and they knew instinctively if any stranger looked suspicious or if any local rogue was up to anything untoward.

Bill Connock, another local character who lived in Bread Street, was very keen that newcomers did not let village standards slip. He hammered on our door one day and berated Sandra – "What are you thinking of Missus? You live opposite the church – there's a funeral going on and you haven't pulled your curtains!"

Marj and Ken Hardacre ran the Crown – you could judge their success by the fact that there was standing room only on Sundays from 12 noon until 3pm. The attraction was darts and shove ha'penny and a very attractive daughter – Pauline! The pub ran an A and B team in each sport and often topped the League with stars like Dennis Carter and his dad, John Pearce, Cyril Langridge et al. Competition for a place was fierce. The slate was widely known for its quality – lovingly tended by Ken with just the right sprinkling of arrowroot. Woe betide anyone who touched it after eating crisps or put a pint within three feet of it!

Weekly lunch hours were an altogether more sedate affair – the corner table by the fire reserved for the 'Sevens' card school – Reece Loxton, Dick Grant, Lye Tucker, Reg Green and anyone else considered fit to join their inner circle. Reece pushed his cycle up Park Hill from his beloved sand beds at the sewage works. Here he dibbed in cuttings surreptitiously snipped with his ex-army clasp knife in his meanders past village gardens. He was also the major source of tomato plants whose seed he got free and gratis from the village night soil – an early example of green recycling. He was often late on parade having stopped to have protracted talks with the Worth twins – little blonde girls – who lived in the house on the hill.

From left: Reece Loxton, Cyril Chapman, Reg Green, Dick Grant

Back row: Ray Norman, Marj Hardacre Stan Atwell, Front row: Brian Hurley, Neville Henderson, Little Billy Symes

Having parked his heavy upright bike against the pub wall, Reece would order his pint of Taunton Cider, take his seat in the corner, open his jack knife and, from a cavernous pocket, produce an enormous handkerchief. Wrapped up in this were a quarter of a cottage loaf and a large lump of very mature Cheddar. On high days and holidays there would also be a slice of prize-winning onion. These never changing comestibles were then sliced, combined and conveyed to his mouth on the broad blade that had, hours before, performed heaven knows what tasks at his place of work!!

Reece was the quietest and gentlest of men. He hardly raised an eyebrow when, as often happened, Lye Tucker reneged 'by accident' when the pot of halfpennies was larger than usual. It was part of the ritual. But Reece could be roused. One summer holiday I had joined the card school – even drinking the obligatory half of cider! We had a new officious village constable who had succeeded in becoming unloved within a fortnight. This day he made an ostentatious entrance to the pub – a man to be reckoned with! He marched up to our table – towered over us and said, "You are breaking the law – Sevens is not on the list of permitted gambling games!"

From left: Cyril Chapman, Reece Loxton, Ray Norman

No one said a word. Lye dealt out the next hand – halfpennies went into the pot. "Did you hear me?" No answer as the play continued. "I said – did you hear me? You are in big trouble if you continue to break the law." Up leapt Reece, a big powerful man who I had never seen move so quickly. His face an inch from the constable's, he spoke in fury but slowly. "Look here, sonny, you bugger off back into Shepton an' tell yer sergeant yer going to arrest us for playing cards and he'll kick yer bloody ass fer us!" Reece slowly sat down breathing heavily. Smiling, Dick Grant dealt the next hand. Exit constable muttering, "Don't let me catch you ever again." In his short stay in the village he was never again to be seen in the pub of a lunchtime.

Last but by no means the least of Pilton worthies was Jack Cox. Jack was a totter in the mould of the Steptoes – a loveable, very minor rogue. One day we saw his truck, loaded with scrap, run down the Shop Lane hill and just about stop by the church gates. Very soon the police arrived – it was alleged that Jack's truck had deficient brakes, no tax, no insurance and a smooth tyre. The outcome was a visit to the Magistrate's Court. Now this may be apocryphal, but when Jack was called in, the local magistrate is supposed to have said, "My goodness! If it isn't Jack Cox my wartime chauffeur." Jack received a caution!

Jack had an aversion or distrust of dentists and doctors bordering on the pathological and a story circulated, however true it was, that, suffering from toothache, he went to his tool shed, found a pair of pliers and pulled out several teeth before he found the right one! I can vouch that he dropped a heavy piece of scrap iron on his arm. He refused to go to Casualty and within days the wound was poisoned, the arm black and swelling, the pain intense. Jack's solution was to

Jack Cox with Tibby

drink brandy day and night in a vain attempt to relieve the symptoms. At last, after much arguing, he was persuaded to let Marj Hardacre dress the suppurating wound. (She was used to dressing shrapnel exit holes in Ken's leg which caused him to suffer great discomfort). Marj dressed Jack's arm faithfully for days, then weeks, until Jack could give up the brandy anaesthetic. I remain convinced that without Marj's care, Jack would have, at the very least, lost his arm.

My final Jack story is of his finely honed sense of mischief and fun. One village gentleman, who often joined the lunch time crowd in the Crown for 'a quick half,' was extremely proud of his roses and, for weeks, kept telling us how he was going to scoop the rose cups at Pilton Show. Jack was no man to miss a challenge. One lunch hour a repeat of the boast was just too much. "Hang on!" says Jack, "What about the rose growing by my front gate up at Hartley Cottages? Tiz a wonder! I digged 'un enormous hole and filled 'er to the brim with the best rotted stuff Reece could give I from down the sewage works." Reece nodded in silent affirmation. "I also got one of Reece's cuttin's what had growed on a bit faster than the rest. T'were that old rambler – Albertine – and I planted 'im in the hole I'd prepared for 'un. Oh, didn't 'e do well? But there be the rub – the reason why I can't beat you at Pilton Show. I'm buggered 'cos it grew and grew in my garden up Hartley but cussed be if 'tisn't *blooming* out at North Wootton!! Blast it – tiz ineligible for Pilton Show!"

Do you know I still have a rose, grown from a certain cutting, from a certain source, growing in my garden? What a surprise after that build up!

If it wasn't snow, there were floods to test the mettle. Sandra Howe recalls:
On Wednesday, July 10th 1968, very heavy rain in Northern France crossed the Channel and arrived in Somerset. It was the biggest storm for 55 years and five inches fell in 24 hours. (Total annual rainfall for this area is about 30 inches). The rain was accompanied by very loud thunder and forked and sheet lightning.

The flood water cascading down Shop Lane threatened to spill over on to our path which led directly down to the front door. Within minutes the ground floor of the cottage would have been underwater. I was very pregnant and had a two year old toddler asleep upstairs. John donned welly boots and strode out into the darkness. The temporary barricade across the path was holding and he knew that our friends at Deepways would fill bags with sand from the children's sandpit. These should hold the water back.

Ten minutes later when he returned home the water at the junction between Shop Lane and St. Mary's Lane had increased in speed and depth and was now reaching the top of his thighs! Armed with sand bags he had to cling onto the stone wall to stop the water from washing him down the hill – a frightening experience in pitch darkness. Several journeys later the temporary barricade supported by the sand bags kept the water out and the house remained safe and dry throughout the night.

The Forsters who lived in Shutwell House were less fortunate. The water from the fields along the A361 poured across the road, down past the telephone box, through their back door and out through their front door. It was four feet deep and caused a lot of damage.

On the same night the bridge across the River Chew at Pensford was completely washed away, as were cottages from which people had to swim for their lives. Pensford was cut off for many days. The army put in a Bailey bridge eventually and it was several years before the bridge was rebuilt. Meanwhile my two year old daughter slept right through the night and woke at the usual time next morning! I think we stayed awake and on watch all night long – the wellies had to be thrown out!

Pilton Flower Show and Fete at Pilton House 1969

In the late '60s, the annual Flower Show and Fete and the Field Day had not yet merged into one event. The first Field Day on the new Playing Fields was held in 1969, purchased for the Parish from the County Council, previously farmed by George Tincknell, "at very favourable rates" according to Philip Eavis. Douglas Turner was Chair of the Field Day Committee. There was a Field Day in 1969, 1970, 1971 before a joint trial event in 1972.

The Flower Show and Fete were held at Pilton House in 1969. The Shepton Mallet Journal records that:

Miss Pilton 1969, Francine Miers of Wincanton, arrived by boat, sailing up an ornamental stream in the grounds of the house, to be crowned by the opener of the fete, Major General A.H.G. Ricketts. While Shepton Mallet town band played *Cruising down the river,* she was rowed around the moat by Nigel Harris.

Then she was piped ashore in true Navy fashion by Commander Brian Fairley, and joined by her maids of honour Elizabeth Strode and Sylvia Butt, chosen at a dance organised by the village Playing Field Committee.

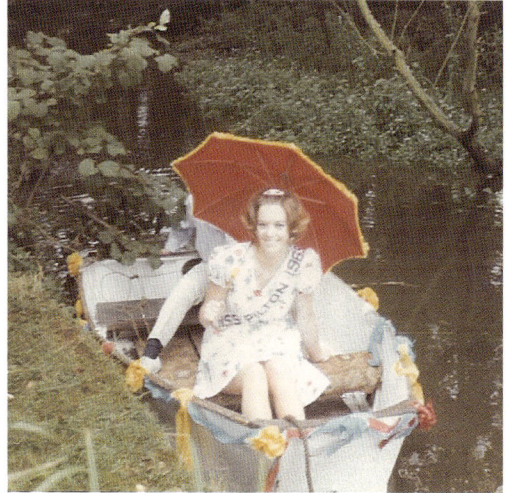

Miss Pilton at the Fete

Miss Pilton at the Fete

Another momentous event happened in 1969, as told me by Margaret Cellan Jones (née Eavis):

Not long before the moon landings, I was driving down Hitchin Hill with Ruth. There was a huge full moon, it was a brilliant, beautiful night.

Coming up the hill, having finished hand milking his couple of cows, walked Fred Chilcot, with a yoke across his shoulders with pails full of milk. He used to milk with a fag in his mouth: so much for health and safety! The cows were kept in small fields between Cumhill and Worthy, known as Straps but no longer there.

We stopped and Ruth asked him what he thought of the idea of sending men to the moon. He looked up at the moon and then said with firm conviction, in his thick Somerset burr, "They'll never get up on he."

Fred Chilcot

On 20th July 1969, the American spacecraft Apollo 11 was the first manned mission to land on the Moon, and Buzz Aldrin and Neil Armstrong took "one small step for man, one giant leap for mankind."

Strange to be writing this when, over 40 years later, a robotic craft named Curiosity has just landed on Mars. One can only wonder what Fred Chilcot would have to say about that.

The 1970s

Poster and ticket for the first Pilton Pop Festival: the Kinks never played but Marc Bolan and T-Rex headlined instead

Radio Times Silver Jubilee Cover 1977 designed by Candace Bahouth

The 1970s were a decade of austerity, power cuts, strikes, the three-day-week, the winter of discontent, decimal currency and joining the Common Market, which Edward Heath said "will affect us whether we go in or stay out."

Yet despite this, the Silver Jubilee of Queen Elizabeth II in 1977 was celebrated nationwide in traditional style.

It was a time of new individualism, of pushing boundaries. In Pilton, the youth revolution arrived when Michael Eavis had his 'road to Damascus' moment by staging the first festival, with free milk, in September 1970. About 1,500 people came, paying £1 a head, which didn't pay off the mortgage on the farm, but helped. The die was cast.

We went over to the Bath Blues Festival on the Bath & West. Funnily enough the bread lady, Eve, who came every morning in a little van, said "Sorry I'm late but I was held up by all these people." "What people?" "Oh, there's a Festival over on the Showground. People everywhere, really weird-looking people." "Really," I said, " that sounds interesting!" So we went and had a look and I thought, this is pretty good. I didn't have a clue what the bread lady was talking about and thought the word 'Festival' was a chapel or church thing. From that very humble, simple beginning...! It was a crazy thing to do but I still did it.

The line-up Michael saw was a roll call of greats: Led Zeppelin, Pink Floyd, Santana, Fairport Convention et al. It inspired him to get on the phone next day, trying but not succeeding to book the Kinks for his planned Festival that September. Instead, Marc Bolan and T-Rex headlined for the first Festival, of which there are plentiful tales in books, souvenir programmes or on websites.
In a film clip from 1970, Michael is shown saying there is a "kind of euphoria down here, it's a nice place for it." *In 2012 he was on a discussion panel on the topic* When did you see the light? *at the Hay Literary Festival. Times have indeed changed beyond recognition for the Methodist farmer.*
Michael continues:

So that was the first one. Some friends of Andrew Kerr's turned up and they said they had a friend who wanted to put on a free festival the next year. So he turned up and he looked pretty good in those days. I came back from Taunton Market and there was Andrew waiting. They didn't like the fact I wasn't a hippy, so they thought I was a bit awkward because I didn't have any truck with them being stoned. With my Methodist background I just couldn't swallow it, really. Funnily enough, they were good company and I enjoyed that.

Andrew had been at the Isle of Wight Festival in August 1970 and, on the way home to London, said: We've got to have a proper festival, one that has some cosmic significance. Let's do it at Stonehenge at the Summer Solstice!

However, having been brought up on a farm I realised that as the land around the stones had acres of corn crops at midsummer, they would be half-grown and unripe. It was obviously very unsuitable to hold a large gathering, especially if most of the crowd would come from the cities untrained in country ways. So what about another sacred site, such as Glastonbury?

...During my search for a site to replace Stonehenge, I received calls from different people telling me about a farmer in Somerset near Glastonbury, who had put on a weekend festival in his fields.

Andrew met Bill Harkin (builder of the first Pyramid Stage) below the Tor after a long sleepless night, the day before meeting Michael for the first time:
I told him of my wish to stage a festival on his farm, which was to be free: a giving event which sought a spiritual awakening and a demonstration against greed. To my surprise he said, "Yes!" He had little hair on his head but it was supported by the 'Newgate Fringe' of a beard so often seen in the rural West Country. He had a broad smile and a beaming face. What I was asking seemed even to me a bit loopy, and for the life of me I cannot imagine why he said, "Yes." Anyway he did, and bless him for it.

Andrew moved into Worthy Farm in October 1970, followed by a colourful and ever-changing cast of more and more people, including Arabella Churchill,

Andrew Kerr in 1971

the following February, who together with Andrew, funded and supported the idea of the free festival. It became a centre for anyone with alternative and New Age, vegetarian or druggy leanings. Some local resentment resulted: "No Hippies Served" signs appeared at the Crown and places in Glastonbury itself. Perhaps not surprising for "A constant stream of visitors arrived, some to help and some to snoop." Tory MP Robert Boscawen introduced a 'Night Assemblies Bill' in Parliament, to try and stop festivals.

Nonetheless, in 1971, Andrew Kerr and Arabella Churchill staged Glastonbury Fair, which was filmed by Nic Roeg, released as 'Glastonbury Fayre.' Andrew had worked for Randolph Churchill, her father and Sir Winston's son. The free festival was fairly chaotic, as Andrew records in his autobiography, 'Intolerably Hip,' from which some extracts follow:
Due to the chaotic nature of the event, there is no exact record of the names of all the bands that played, but it is fairly sure that all of these did.

There followed a lengthy list, the highlight perhaps might have been David Bowie on Saturday night but timings overran and he eventually played at dawn. He returned to headline the Pyramid Stage with a memorable set in 2000.

First Pyramid Stage 1971

Bill Harkin built the first Pyramid Stage for 1971, on a spot dowsed by Andrew and another dowser. Bill had a dream, after which he scribbled a sketch showing the pyramid shape. At the time John Michell had written the inspirational 'View Over Atlantis' and was very keen on Glastonbury and ancient sacred geometry. He advised Andrew to base the stage on the dimensions within Stonehenge: his calculations resulted in a scaled version of the Great Pyramid. Michael Eavis said, "So suddenly Glastonbury was a huge thing and it wasn't about Pilton any more."

Nonetheless, a framework for future festivals appears to have been established, not least with the iconic stage. Sound was a problem, as Andrew recalls:

...the purple speaker system was very powerful. It seemed to gather all of the sound and take it out of the valley and dump it right into the village. Listening from the road behind the church I could understand the complaint and asked for the sound to be turned down. The other problem was that it went on until well after midnight. The generator was going 24 hours a day until its carer apologised, saying that it was overheating and needed a rest.

...Michael, being the landowner, became the butt of complaints. He must have thought the film company was at fault. I watched him and Jean chasing an assistant director around in the forest of scaffolding beneath the stage. The quarry, with great presence of mind did a quick turnaround, deftly removed his baseball cap and donned a wig and sauntered slowly back to meet them and pass unnoticed.

...From time to time, we would go down through the crowd to the pyramid and watch bands from the side of the stage. Melanie's set stole the show for me, and she stole many hearts as well. Her *Peace Will Come* was so moving. I also especially remember Fairport Convention. I was not there for Arthur Brown's astounding performance ending with burning crosses. That upset a few sensitive people. Another favourite was Brinsley Schwarz: halfway through their set, a crowd of followers of the 14 year old Indian boy, Prem Rawat, known to devotees as Guru Maharaji, flooded the stage, ejected the band and set up a very ancient chair from the farmhouse, which Michael had bought from his neighbour Teddy Stone. The Guru removed his shoes, sat in it and addressed the audience below.

I was horrified and left the stage. He was dressed in a white suit that seemed to glow as I passed him. I heard that it was not a very good experience for the boy Guru, who had only been in the country a few days and his first public appearance anywhere outside India. Walking through the crowd I heard him say there should be an end to all sex. However, later, I discovered that he had in fact said 'sects.'

Andrew, now in his 70s, has retired to Pilton after living in Scotland and Italy and numerous other adventures.

Rev Walker's son, Tim remembers this time:
In the early '70s, there was quite a stir at the Christmas midnight mass when the first of the hippies came in, late, during *Once in Royal David's City,* the first carol. The church was packed but the music stopped and everyone turned around, when these exotic creatures in huge long fur coats and Russian fur hats came through the door!

Others moved west who weren't hippies but wanted to experience a new life away from the city. Candace and John Fletcher came to Pilton in 1971 and Candace, American by birth, with Palestinian and Italian parents, describes the culture shock:
When I first came to Pilton – an arbitrary choice on our part – it just happened Ebenezer Chapel was available. John would be in the country during the week and I'd come at weekends. He stayed in Glastonbury to begin with and we'd been looking at various places. Because he was a writer and I was an artist, we couldn't get a mortgage but we had just a little bit of cash. From London, where we stayed with his parents, we kept on looking further and further out. Pilton did seem very rural to me but I was up for this adventure. We came to the Chapel and it reminded me of New York 'lofts' with plenty of space. Because we'd been looking at tiny dark cottages with low ceilings, I loved it, even though we did have a sitting tenant. That was Ella Blacker, before that it was Mrs Fletcher (no relation) who reached 100.

The Chapel was deconsecrated when we bought it. We met the Trustees, who were Michael, Philip, Colin Rose and Mr Connock, who had coffins down in the cellar, which had been the Sunday School. Michael seemed quite keen on us coming to the village.

The coffins eventually had to go and I do remember a Hells' Angel turned up and took one off to use as a sidecar.

Ella was in the cottage. It had no bathroom. The bathroom was just the outside loo. It had some kind of hot water or laundry thing, a brick thing in the back kitchen. She was given an old people's bungalow.

At first, we stayed in a caravan at Mr Strickland's, that's where I met Ray Loxton. So we moved in and had the cottage done but not the Chapel, that stayed with the pews in for a while. For a while, I was weaving in a plastic tent in the middle, as it was so cold at times: the Chapel wasn't done for some time.

Josie, Bessie and Frank Hiscox were across the road. Then Andrew Kerr came and made that stone wall entrance for them.

John was teaching at Millfield and in the summer he was making hay with Met Bown. I used to go down to Michael's every morning with a small churn to get milk, dunk it into the big vat. At lunchtime I'd walk all the way down to Sticklynch (I can't believe I did this!) and we'd have a picnic under an apple tree.

I was the only American for quite a while and now there are four. When I first came I remember Mr Garland at the Forge at North Wootton. When he found out I was American he sort of stepped back, and then when he found out I was Catholic – he stepped back even further, horrified. It was like I was an alien!

In 1971 for the Glastonbury Fair, as I remember, we were in the caravan at Stricklands. A friend of ours came back with a garland of flowers in her hair. When John came back, Mr Strickland chased him with a pitchfork around the farmyard and shouted at him for being "down there with them hippies."

It was quite a culture shock and I think took about five years to adjust. Still, I loved it. To me it was so much more rural then than now. We were the first 'blow-ins.'

Given her exotic lineage and looks, Candace was enlisted to read palms at Pilton Fete, held in the grounds of Pilton House. In this photo from the early '70s, she reads Kathleen Milne's hand, in an old caravan.

Ebenezer Chapel had originally been built specifically for the people who built the railway line in the 19th century, a kind of mission place to serve them. Philip Eavis describes: It closed in the mid 1960s and the two congregations merged, the Ebenezer and the Wesleyan, after a lot of argy bargy, with which I was much involved. Very unpopular and contentious. I was very pro the Union of these two Societies. There was opposition particularly from the Ebenezer side, being the smaller church. The key person to see it through was Charlie Rose, senior steward of the Ebenezer.

The first combined Pilton Day, consisting of a trial merger of the Field Day and the Flower Show and Fete, was held in 1972. Douglas Turner was Chairman of the Field Day and Dick Bethell was titular Chairman but unable to attend on the day as it conflicted with a sheep Show! In those days, John Howe was also involved. For 1973 it went back to separate shows, but according to Philip Eavis: Since '72 went so well, everyone knew that was the way forward. So in 1974 we decided to join up and call it Pilton Day. No longer the Field Day, the Flower Show, but Pilton Day. George Windsor played a pivotal part in persuading the Legion to take that course of action. Because there was a lot of opposition in 1971 when we decided to try it, they thought this upstart Eavis and Co. were moving too fast.

Philip was later to become Chairman for many many years, but as he says: a great many people play an equally as important role, if not more, in making the Show work.

John Fletcher writes:
When I moved to Pilton in 1971, I worked for Metford Bown, a farmer down at Sticklynch. His farm adjoined the by then disused Somerset & Dorset railway line, on the other side of which was a large pond. All of this has now disappeared beneath the new by-passy road which sweeps past the Apple Tree Inn.

During the mid-70s, at Pilton Day, Joanna Benner was voted Miss Pilton, wearing a velvet dress from Biba.

It was haymaking. I was working in the field next to the pond, raking in the outside swarf so that the baler could pick it up. Looking over the hedge I saw that a few hippies had come down the railway track from the festival and were bathing in the pond.

Mr Bown turned up. He started following me along the swarf driving a large tractor and even larger baler. Suddenly he looked over the hedge. At that moment a beautiful and entirely naked hippie girl arose like Venus from the waves and walked toward the railway line. Metford Bown was a man entirely innocent of the modern world. Even in the hottest weather he wore at least four layers of clothes. His mouth fell open. He stared and stared. The tractor and the baler went smack into the ditch. It took us quite a time to get them out.

Met Bown was born in the 1910s, somewhere I think in East Town. His uncle farmed a farm in Sticklynch. When he was 14 his uncle offered him a job on his farm for life, promising to leave him the farm in his will, provided he never married.

Metford had just started courting a girl over the hill, but times were hard and he took the job. His uncle lived well into his 90s. He didn't die until the late '60s. The courting had continued secretly for 40 years. A week after his uncle's death they got married. They were together a year. I started working for them in that yard.

Then she died. Being a farmer he took it stoically. He didn't say a thing. He came out and did the morning milking. Only then, after we'd completely finished clearing up, did he announce that he'd found his wife dead.

He lived for another ten years. He died in a traditional country way. When told he was ill he turned his face to the wall and seven days later he was dead.

During the '70s, Ray Loxton, hedgelayer and countryman, known for his attitude to the land he loves, "The good Lord put me here and everywhere I survey I go," *remembers a time when he fell foul of a local landowner, while exercising a ferret*: I looked up and was surprised to see someone there. "Who gave you permission to be on my land?" he asked. I had to think quick and I said that Mr Turner had told me it was OK. "We had better check that with him," said the Colonel and from behind the hedge stepped Mr Turner. "Who is it?" he asked, "Ah, young Loxton. Well, I remember saying you could catch rabbits on my land but I don't remember ..." At this point I thought it best to explain I'd made a mistake and go on my way. As I left I heard the landowner shout, "And never darken my woods again!" as the ferret bit deep into my finger.

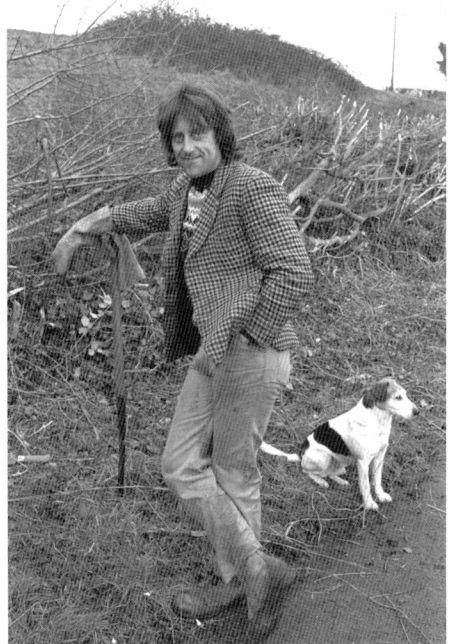

Ray Loxton looking the part

Rob Kearle relates another tale of Ray's exploits, which must have been before the above tale:
Ray was caught with a brace of pheasants slung over his shoulder in Burford Woods. Colonel Bond said to him, "What are you doing poaching in my woods?" "I ain't poaching, I'm out for a walk." "What are those, then?" pointing to the pheasants. Ray turned round to look at the birds, recoiled comically and jumped, "Aargh – how did they get there?" James Bond and George Windsor, who was with him, collapsed with laughter and let him go, with the invisible pheasants.

Rob Kearle recalls schooldays at West Pennard:

At West Pennard School, because I couldn't read or write very well as I was dyslexic, the village mothers such as Hilary and Ruth would come and help with reading and I remember years later Hilary Austin saying she actually fell asleep because I was so boring reading! They dedicated an enormous amount of their time helping other people, and still do. I had no interest in it aged six or seven. I've still got the piano that used to be played at school assembly, that somehow Tod Morris-Adams had.

My one resounding memory of early childhood is all the elm trees, because I lived at Elm Farm, all these massive elm trees. Then all these huge blokes with massive chainsaws cutting down the dead trees, which seemed to go on for ever. Day after day, week after week, year after year, chopping them all down, chopping them all up. That was Dutch Elm Disease. Obviously, trees are one of my big things, and I survey and look after all the trees on the Festival site but when I look back to the 1971 film of the Festival, I can't recognise anywhere, because of the huge elm trees. Whereas now we look at the site and go, that lovely big oak tree or that ash, I can't recognise the fields before, because of the huge elms.

It didn't start hitting here until well into the mid '70s. I remember these mammoth trees, which is where my interest in trees comes from. Then the unbelievable change in the landscape, as big as the Agricultural Revolution, as big as the Enclosure Act.

Elms were called 'widow makers' because they had this habit of big limbs just falling off, for no reason. Farm workers used to sit under the trees for lunch and breaks and a big three tonne branch would fall down. So they were known locally as widow makers. Elm was also used for coffin boards.

In 1973 a true villager, Alice Miell, passed away: Ruth Eavis says she owes her love of flowers and knowledge of wildflowers to Auntie Alice. John Fletcher wrote this tribute to her at the time:

In a hedgerow she could tell a Tufted Vetch
from a Bush Vetch, giving both
English and Latin names;
She could milk a cow and teach a child,
Her damson jam was always the best in Pilton;
She tended bees for their honey and
Could quote Milton from the heart
And Trollope from the tongue;
She held her opinions and hosannahed her psalms
– she was a good competent woman.

What I remember most vividly was reading to her from Milton's vast poem *Paradise Lost*. One time I looked at her and thought she'd fallen asleep – her eyes had shut and her false teeth rested on her lower lip. Then I realized she was concentrating. Her teeth clicked back into place and she started repeating exactly, word for word, what I was reading. She knew the whole poem by heart.

Auntie Alice in her penny hat, sketched by Candace

Jenny de Gex writes:

When my parents moved here in 1974 they were told there would never be another Festival: little did they know it would grow and grow into the giant it is today. Various disgruntled 'antis' wanted my father to join them but he refused to do so, being far more fascinated by the machines Mendip Council installed to measure the sound decibels, which he called 'noisometers' and would keep checking them, as if they were weather barometers.

John Cooper Clarke, the punk poet, currently enjoying a revival, I remember enraged the village, but that may have been later. Olive Linsley and friends wrote to the newspapers complaining, as every single f-word could clearly be heard up here in the village. Clearly no one had thought of turning the sound down, or away from the village, as happens now.

My family moved to Pilton because they knew the Bethells and McNeills of old, and were trying to find somewhere 'west of Newbury.' Thank goodness they came this far west instead, as it was a happy twist of fate that landed them here, in all respects. The year they moved here, I was in Bristol where a friend was working and we came out for a picnic on the edge of the Mendips. At that breathtaking view from Deer Leap, with the Tor a mere dot below, surrounded by the patchwork landscape striped by rhynes and the Bristol Channel shimmering silver, I had a very strong feeling of coming home, infused by the power of such natural beauty. Within six months, this became home, although until the '90s I split time elsewhere. Sadly neither parent lived into ripe old age to enjoy Somerset for as long as I have been lucky enough to do. Yet we had ancestors in Frome, Bath and on the Quantocks and Dartmoor, so it was meant to be.

In the early to mid '70s, as well as being a centre of hippiedom, the village was also known as the 'Elephant's Graveyard' as it boasted several high-ranking military officers. Possibly the greatest of them, Lieutenant-General Sir Brian Horrocks, KCB, KBE, DSO, MC was more reclusive, although he gave the prizes at Pilton Day one year. After a distinguished wartime career, described by Eisenhower as "an outstanding British general under Montgomery," he latterly wrote history and presented TV programmes and was Black Rod in the House of Lords for 14 years.

Others had known each other for many years and would get together for pheasant shooting at Burford, nothing like as well-organised as today. Jeannie McNeill describes how her father noted in a shooting diary: that they got one pheasant, two rabbits, had eight assorted unruly dogs and ten small bedraggled children, but a wonderful lunch was had afterwards at the Bonds. I always remember them, not much shooting but a wonderfully wet day out.

Jeannie noted that in the latter part of her parents' time in Pilton, especially when her mother was on her own: people would check that she drew and opened the curtains, did shopping for her, took the dog out for walks and all those wonderful things that constitute a true village.

Christopher Bond writes about his father, Colonel (as opposed to Commander) James Bond, who inherited Burford House in 1970:
He married his wife Joan shortly after his evacuation from Dunkirk. Thinking Hitler was about to invade England, my mother put her most precious possession (her wedding dress) inside a cushion which we found 50 years later. He was a brave man and was decorated with the Military Cross for building a Bailey Bridge under enemy fire at the bloody battle of Monte Cassino in Italy; 30 years later he found it still in use as a road, so it must have been well built. After being stationed abroad in Egypt and Malta and living in Monmouth Castle, where Henry V was born, he retired to live at Burford with my grandmother, Amy. He established a chicken farm of thousands of egg-producing birds, building the houses himself. This employed people living in Burford and Pilton. He restarted the Burford Valley Shoot, with Generals, Brigadiers and Colonels as the guns. He enjoyed golf and died on Burnham Golf Course from a heart attack.

My memories of him were as a kind, fair but shy man. The War shaped those who fought in it, and it is difficult to imagine how they might otherwise have been. He was a Church Warden and Treasurer at Pilton for many years. An early adapter to the computer, on his death there were concerns about how to recover the accounts from his prototype machine.

As he became older he decided to sell Burford House in two parts (now two modernized large homes) and rebuild the coach house and stables there. Using his engineering knowledge, he demolished everything within the exterior walls and built a comfortable, wind-tight modern house inside, where we now live. At that time, he sold most of Old Burford Farm to Stephen Turner, but retained the woodland.

The old chicken houses at Burford continue to provide invaluable storage space for all the stalls for Pilton Show; the woodland is now a modern organised shoot during the season. The gardens have been lovingly restored and now open annually under the National Gardens Scheme.

Rob Kearle recalls how his brother Danny found evidence of wild boar at Burford:
Danny and Bill Burroughs cleared out a well right on top of Burford Hill, between Burford and West Compton on the ridge back towards Elm Farm. There was a huge deep well, which clearly had mechanisms for a wind powered extraction system in there. It was full of the bones of wild boar. Burford Woods used to have wild boar in there for a long time. Clearly when they butchered the boars, they put all the bones down the well. This was 40 years ago.

Hilary Austin describes how their family moved in 1975:
For many years we were known as the family in the 'New House.' We were quite relieved when more houses were built and we were no longer the newest arrivals, especially when we learnt that the house should been a bungalow! Fortunately we had nothing to do with the building of it. We were quickly made to feel at home when John Walker arrived the day we moved in, parked in the middle of the road and joined us for a cup of tea. Passing motorists, or those trying to pass, were probably less pleased. When we got to know him better, we realised that this was quite the normal way of parking.

   We soon became involved in village life and were quickly seen as prospective helpers for Pilton Show. For our family, the Show became the highlight of the year and some of us became quite competitive! However, it was perhaps the evening Barn Dance we most looked forward to, for as well as an evening of fun for all the family, it also meant that younger members were allowed to stay up beyond their normal bedtime. Now they don't need permission to do so but like many families in the village, they still return for Pilton Day and the Barn Dance, bringing with them friends they have met over the years, who now also mark the first Saturday in September in their diaries. James has a special reason to mark the event, because it was at the Barn Dance that he met his future wife, so it was appropriate, when they decided to get engaged, that they should do so at the Barn Dance on Pilton Day.

The Austin Family in 1987

Rebecca is the only member of the family who can pass as a true Piltonian, having been born and married here but for the rest of the family, we still like to feel that we belong here.

Kate (Katheryn) Austin recalls how special the ford is for her, down memory lane:
The ford is where in 1976, shortly after moving in, my brother, sister and I went 'swimming.' Quite a fun thing to do: one of us had fallen in and the others thought we would join them, fully clothed in winter coats and welly boots. I am told we created something of an unusual first impression in the village.

I spent many hours there with siblings and friends, and often simply by myself, dangling my legs over the bridge watching the water flow on its way. We built dams, hunted creatures under stones, threw large rocks into the water to create ripples and soak the others. We dared one another to

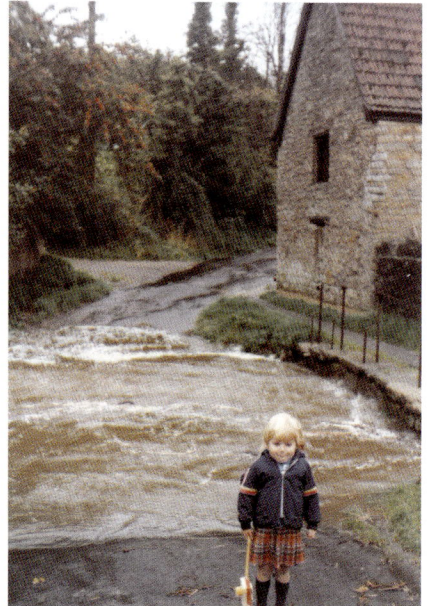

Rebecca Austin, Kate's sister, at the ford in 1980

venture under the bridge – a sport no longer possible due to the netting, probably a good thing. Only occasionally did we venture further upstream, and never again after a polite telling off from the residents of a certain house!

I recall walking home without shoes and socks, trying to keep to the verge to avoid the sharp stones in the road. I also remember egging Dad on to go faster and faster as he drove the car through the ford – he didn't need much encouragement! I can also think of times when the usually gently flowing ford became a raging torrent and ran close to, or right over, the top of the bridge.

As I grew up, the ford and nearby footpaths provided quiet locations to take romantic rambles! It was also a place with many shadows when walking home from a friend's house having watched a late night horror film. I always requested to be escorted home after that.

I crossed the ford with my husband as we walked to church to celebrate our marriage on a scorching summer's day in July 1999. I would have loved to have joined my father and father-in-law, who navigated the shallow waters of the ford itself via a series of stepping stones. However I'm sure if I had I would have fallen prey to the benign-looking, but incredibly slippery, edges of the ford, and a wet wedding dress would probably *not* have been a good look!

Now we bring our two children to Pilton to visit their grandparents, and a trip is not complete without an outing to the ford. They would both happily spend hours building dams, and throwing stones just as I did. For me it remains a place of quiet contemplation, as well as somewhere I might receive an occasional soaking, courtesy of a well-aimed stone thrown by my son or one of his cousins.

In the 1970s, English wine was undergoing a revival and Nigel and Anne Godden had planted vines at Pilton Manor in 1966 and 1968. Harvesting was in September or October and in April 1976 a national colour supplement featured British viticulture on their cover, with a feature by Prue Leith.

Nigel Godden at Pilton Manor

Lunch for grape pickers in the courtyard at Pilton Manor 1975

I can vouch for Fred Swingler's impressions of 'le Pick,' having harvested in 1975 for said feature above:

Having worked in the wine trade for 20 odd years, I was delighted to move to Pilton in 1976 as the village had its very own vineyard. In the late summer of that year I knocked on the yard door of Pilton Manor House and met Nigel and Anne Godden and asked if they needed any help with grape picking. "Of course, of course – always happy to have an extra pair of hands. Late September probably this year – bring your own secateurs."

The vintage was great fun and the pickers were a really nice crowd – mostly villagers with a few from Glastonbury. We worked in pairs both sides of each row, placing the bunches into black plastic buckets which, when full, were tipped into large tubs to be driven to the press at the Manor.

A super Italian fellow, named Angelo, was in charge of fermentation. All the grapes were of green varieties – mostly Mueller Thurgau – a German hybrid.

Lunch was provided and was an amazing affair on long trestle tables in the main courtyard with *lasagna* or stuffed vine leaves and plenty, and I mean plenty, of their own delicious white wine.

My wife, Libby, was roped in and we both enjoyed working together, only very occasionally darting for the same bunch of grapes and jabbing each other's hands with our secateurs! Once, when the weather turned really bad, all the others went home but we decided to stay and complete our row and Nigel and Anne gave us lunch in their kitchen. Eventually, lunches were held in the hospitality unit and, after the Goddens sadly left, ceased altogether. Libby and I have very fond memories indeed of those early times.

Trudie Reilly, mother of Andy, Sean and Sheelagh Allen, was there during the grape harvest, so Liz Elkin's appreciation of her is a fitting tribute:
Trudie loved playing skittles and cards. "Whist means 'whist ye noise' so keep quiet," she advised when we played. She also loved Lyme Regis, Jim Reeves and a glass of Chablis with friends. An invitation to help her tidy up last year's Christmas drinks so she could buy (or win at whist drives) ready for this year would occasionally lead us into trouble but never Trudie. She liked soaps on TV, *steak au poivre* and *crème brûlée*. She enjoyed a robust discussion on many subjects but if you had all night to spare it was worth bringing football or the Liberals into the conversation. One can only imagine how much Chablis would be required to discuss the Coalition with Trudie in that vineyard in the sky.

Ladies skittles 24 hour fundraiser for Pilton Working Men's Club to build new skittle alley,' 76/77
Back row *from L to R: George Blacker, Eileen Hiscox, Trudie Reilly, Sheelagh Allen,*
Carol Mackay, Phyllis Higgins, Audrey Brown, Marylin Pearce, Ivy Fleming, Margaret Vickery,
Gill Vickery, Doreen Cox.
Frontrow: *Eileen Govier, Jackie Fleming, Nicky Gregory, Christine Reilly, Margaret Windsor*

In 1976, novelist Fay Weldon and her antique dealer and artist husband Ron moved to Orchardleigh, or what we affectionately called 'Weldonia.' Several of her novels were set in Somerset, or inspired thereby, including 'Puffball' (later filmed by aforementioned Nic Roeg, produced by Fay's son Dan), 'The Heart of the Country' (for which some locals were extras in the TV version). She has been Chairman of the judges for the Booker Prize, as well as shortlisted for 'Praxis.' Her fiction, which includes novels, five collections of short stories, and a number of plays written for TV, radio and the stage, typically portrays contemporary women trapped in oppressive situations caused by the patriarchal structure of society. Her incisive mind and wit remain as sharp today, despite the passing of the years.

Fay's son Dan Weldon, now a writer, filmmaker and teacher of media studies, recalls what it was like growing up in the '70s in Somerset:

We arrived from London in 1976 in that hot, hot summer. I was 11 years old. I had come from a big inner city school in Pimlico to Whitstone in Shepton Mallet – a much smaller school where they talked weird. I felt like an alien… I probably was an alien… and it is a feeling that has stayed my whole adult life. Thank you, Shepton. Shepton Mallet is linked to Pilton for me, one led to the other. Sorry but I'll have start with Shepton.

Shepton Mallet is defined by its past. My Gran's theory was that the Roman lead mines made Shepton mad – the lead seeped into the drinking water and left its mark for centuries, and I think she was right. Oliver Cromwell liked soldiers from Shepton because their eyes rolled in their heads and they terrified Royalists – a Sheptonian in Bruton is like a donkey in a Brahmin village, try it and see, it'll end in tears.

Our games teacher at Whitstone, a bully, was definitely a victim of Roman lead. I didn't like him. And it must have been the Roman lead that made the council tear down its medieval heart and to twin itself with Misberg, a town we bombed in the war, that as far as I can tell is famous for cement. Shepton Mallet invented Babycham… the place is clearly insane.

On the upside, Shepton Mallet had a famous matador, and a prison not famous enough for executing black GI's in the war. One of them fell in love with a white girl from Bath and it took 30,000 locals to petition Eisenhower to save the man's life. Then there's Cannards Grave, with a pub that marks the spot of another executed man, this time for sheep stealing; a pub where I was attacked in 1978 around the head and stomach for wearing a 'poof's' earring. At the police station to press charges against my attacker the desk sergeant – you know who you are – threw me against a wall and said I was a commie drug dealer and I should 'watch my back.' I was 13 and felt rather flattered. I was like Clyde without a Bonnie.

Not long after I had a date with a possible Bonnie. She was lovely, we walked around the prison walls in the fog, had four *Babychams* in the band stand and a snog and chips from the 'chinky' on the Market Cross before her dad came to pick her up at 10.15. He turned out to be the desk sergeant and I had to hide in the graveyard for an hour as he hunted me down (a rather wonderful graveyard as it happens, attached to an amazing church overshadowed by that brutalist building …madness). I'd have to go further afield to find my Bonnie and that's how I discovered Pilton… an autumnal, moonlit kiss on the porch of Pilton church; there were bats and owls and she wore '70s velvet. Thanks to the horrors of Shepton, Pilton was my coming of age.

There is no lead in Pilton, thankfully. You discover Pilton by chance. It hides in a valley and attracts people who don't want to be seen. Pilton is a place of myth and mystery and radical Methodists. As a teenager I was at ease in Pilton, and so what if they think that Joseph of Arimathea came to visit in a boat with a staff and a toddler whose mother was a virgin? It's absurd, where's the port? John Fletcher told me this story and he made it sound plausible but he was good at that, wasn't he?

And did those feet in ancient time
Walk upon England's mountain green?
And was the holy Lamb of God
On England's pleasant pastures seen?

Well, Blake believed the story too and I've just realised he's talking about Pilton, Pilton is Jerusalem and Shepton Mallet the dark satanic mills… it's obvious. And I suppose if enough people believe it, then it must be true. Pilton does that to you… the present defines history, not the other way around.

Dan Weldon also remembers, in the late '70s and early '80s:
Sitting in Ruth Eavis's kitchen for debates well into the early hours, post Rifleman's, around the kitchen table – tea, biscuits, more tea… discussions like 'Should men with learning difficulties be allowed prostitutes on the National Health?' Ruth was in the chair overseeing with wisdom and compassion and shrieks of enthusiasm. Becky, Jane, Juliet, their assorted boyfriends and then there was Robert Owens (who I miss so much) and lovely Anna and many more whose names I can't remember but whose faces are etched into my brain. Politics, religion, ethics and quality gossip. I learnt about things they didn't teach at school. Someone, who I won't name, thought all girls had their periods on the same day each month at the same time: he was dealt swift and sympathetic blows, although my understanding at the time that bees made honey and wasps made jam was never exposed, thank God.

Dan remembers Bourne Farm in midsummer:

I had a holiday job with Steven Corfield on his organic farm, when to be organic was eccentric, not like now. I remember Danny Kearle, Shire horses, vintage tractors and haymaking with a very fat man and a flagon of cider – or did I dream that? Having not worked on a farm before, I thought all farms were like this. Sadly not: there was a kid at school who took me to the farm that his dad managed, it was a factory and everything was for profit. It had no soul.

For Steven I worked very hard for 10 pence an hour, I think I came cheap to be honest, but the memories are vitally strong in my life and when things get tough and pointless, as they do, I think, get a farm and buy a horse and I might just do it one day. I remember hot days in June calling in the cows, I'd just open the gate and 'Queenie' the boss cow would lead the herd down East Town Lane to the milking parlour. They were beautiful Jersey cows with dreamy eyes and they even defecated elegantly, more of a PHFFFFUTPLUMP than a FARRFLOPFFFLOPSPLAT!

I also worked occasionally for Michael at Worthy Farm – he paid better. I'd do Steven in the morning and Michael in the afternoon, or at least that's how I remember it – maybe it only happened a few times, but I'd walk slowly and alone down East Town Lane to Worthy Farm on a hot day… the flowers, the insects, the smell, the melting tarmac, the soft bit in the long grass to chew, the swallows swooping… and the sounds… it was impossible to feel alone.

And on this walk I'd meet people… I remember talking to Jenny de Gex's dad in his garden about serious and interesting things. I don't remember what was said but I do remember him taking the time to talk to me, a 14 year old, as an equal. Not many adults do that, and I think about this with my own children. I remember he had a handsome black Labrador that sat patiently and seemed to listen too.

I remember cider making at Worthy Farm: lots of men and Lurchers and apples and straw and did John Fletcher wear Plus Fours? I know he had an old Rover 90 that smelt of petrol and leather and I remember Michael playing Elgar to his cows, he claimed it made them happier. Happy or not I've liked Elgar ever since and when I hear *Nimrod* now I think of udders, not England. Thank you Michael.

I won't talk about the Festival because for me Pilton isn't the Festival. It is a vast city that rises and falls each year and it is separate somehow. But I do love it, of course I do, it made my teenage life so exciting – although I did see a woman give birth in a tree on acid and find a man who'd somehow fallen through the toilet hole into the pooh pit (he was naked except for one of those horrible biker's leather hats you can only buy in Wales). I so wish I hadn't seen that.

I could go on and on: the memories are alive and kicking. And strangely I don't have one photograph. Just images in my head.

But the last word, because it has just come into my head, has to go to the shop at the bottom of the hill. I can't remember the names of the two women that ran it but they sold *Orange Maids* and frozen cherry *Jubblies*. They also sold single *Embassy Kingsize* out of a glass behind the counter and they asked no questions. Lovely *Jubblies*.

My father died in 1995 and we all left – my Gran, my brothers, my sister, my niece, my nephews, my mother and me. But somehow it is all still there playing itself out… on England's Green and Pleasant Land just down the road from the Satanic Mills.

Steven Corfield later formed Serious Stages*, providing imaginatively designed stages for festivals, concerts and events all over the world.*

John Fletcher worked for another local farmer, Owen Boyce, who would appear at Ebenezer Chapel every week with potatoes and flowers, with a wet roll-up cigarette hanging as if glued to his lip:
At the end of the 1970s Owen Boyce was getting quite old (I'm not sure if at any time in his life he looked under 60). His smallholding in West Compton had become overrun – a bit like my garden now – and he asked me if I'd like to do a week's work tidying it up. I agreed not because I expected to get paid vast sums – the average wage then was about £30 a week and Owen *was* a farmer – but because he was a friend and becoming quite frail.

So I started – scything nettles, docking docks, cutting back brambles, relaying barbed wire fences. He gave me as much help as his body would allow, but he mainly stood around reminiscing and rolling me extremely thin cigarettes from his tobacco. Always wearing a black Gallic beret.

There was an upside to this job, though. I got fed sumptuously at lunchtime by his wife Mrs Boyce – rabbit pies, vegetables fresh from the garden, puddings with lashings of cream. (Mrs Boyce was mainly famous for having issued forth into her farmyard during a Second World War air raid wearing a saucepan on her head as a helmet. She also had an extremely loud voice. It was quite possible when having a phone call with her to stand on the other side of the room to the phone and hear every word she said. Ruth Eavis is the only other person I know who can do this).

So it was a very pleasant week. I rehung gates, burnt rubbish, and piled up bales of hay. But all the time I noticed Owen getting ever more slightly distant from me.

Finally Friday came. The meal was wonderful. Beetroots, bacon and liver, great fat spuds. It lasted two hours. Owen and I went out to do the final tidying up. But all the time I sensed him getting more and more nervous. Finally it was finished. It was time to pay me. He mumbled a few words, pressed something hurriedly into my hand and then, ancient as he was, executed a miraculously swift scissors leap over an adjoining barbed wire fence and was halfway across the next field before I even had time to look down into my hand. There lay a £5 note. A five pound note!!

What is it about farmers and money?

The Queen's Silver Jubilee was cause for national celebration in 1977 and Pilton was not to be left out. The Hon. Mrs Fraser who was on the organising committee, received a telegram from Buckingham Palace, worded thus: The Queen sincerely thanks the Parishioners of Pilton for their kind and loyal message on the occasion of Her Majesty's Silver Jubilee.

Candace Bahouth (professional name) was commissioned to do the front cover of the Radio Times, *in a weaving she still has today. In the '70s she became friendly with pop artist Peter Blake, who was coincidentally commissioned to do the 2012 Diamond Jubilee cover.*

Radio Times Silver Jubilee cover 1977

Village celebrations consisted of a church service, a street party all along Bread Street, for which the sun fortunately shone and a revival of the football match in drag, staged this time on the Playing Fields. Additionally, on a memorably cold evening, there was a pageant at Burford: John Barkle was, as ever, in fine voice.

Street party in Bread Street

John Barkle in Jubilee pageant at Burford

Jubilee football match in drag repeating the Coronation idea

John Fletcher

81

Bread was still made in the village, as Sandra Howe recalls:
Burnside, now a house in Bakery Lane, was the village bakery. We were always tempted when we walked past by the incredible smell of freshly baked bread.

The high spot of the day for many of the village children was getting off the school bus on Top Street, being met by their mothers and asked if they had been good children? Of course, they swore that they had and the reward for this was to go home the long way round, taking them down Barrow Lane across the road and into Bakery Lane. There they presented themselves at the door of the bakery and, if they were lucky and there were any left, they were the recipients of hot, scrumptious, sugary, jammy doughnuts! These they carried back home in a paper bag along the river path with the grease dripping out all through Weir Lane. The doughnuts went down very well as a pre-tea extra. Eve, who many of you may remember, drove the van to deliver our bread and she was always willing to chat and pass on the latest news. At our house, she had to watch our cat, who, at the first opportunity would jump into the van and greedily devour any bun he could get his claws into: sometimes he was successful!

In 1978 as part of the Pilton Day weekend, there was a concert Summer's End at Pilton, *at which the Bevan Family Choir sang, with Gillian Knight, who then lived at the Bush, singing solos by Bizet, Gluck and Handel. The following week she was soloist at the Last Night of the Proms at the Albert Hall! A mezzo soprano, she sang regularly at the Royal Opera House in Covent Garden and sometimes kindly gave my mother and myself tickets, after which we'd go backstage. Her daughter is now one of the Opera Babes.*

In 1979, Arabella Churchill and Bill Harkin staged 'The Year of the Child' Festival at Worthy Farm. She then remained involved with all following Festivals until her untimely death in 2007. As Michael said "She was a bit of a shining light." *From then onwards, informal gigs happened at the Wagon Shed on the farm, before application for a licence was granted to hold a larger scale event, the first Glastonbury Festival for CND in 1981.*

In 1979, the Happy Circle Club was formed by the WRVS (Women's Royal Voluntary Services) who took 'meals on wheels' around the community. They thought it would be a good idea if older villagers could meet regularly. The club, no longer affiliated to the WRVS, has come a long way since then, meeting for talks, meals, outings. Ena Grant thought of the name Happy Circle.

Philip Eavis increasingly concentrated on retail rather than farming in this decade: Consumer Buyers had begun in 1965 from a building at Benleigh, with the repair workshops and storage in the old buildings that were part of Hazeldene Farm.

In 1977 Living Homes opened in Street and "although it started in Pilton, I hope it will be going on for many generations." *In the following decade he became increasingly involved with local Liberal politics, the former offices of Consumer Buyers becoming campaign HQ, as well as the police command post during the Festival, until it moved downhill to be on site, as numbers increased.*

Local parish politics became increasingly complex, as Philip described:
Charlie Boyce had the awful job of being the District Councillor in the '70s and he was the person who took all the stick for the Festival. He was as much involved in the birth pangs in a way as Michael, because he was trying to pacify everybody. People accused him of not taking sides because he was a pragmatic, consensus kind, trying to work it out. He had a hell of a time. He was trying to handle the situation. Although he was a true blue Conservative, he was always an independent Councillor. In the end, the party asked him to stand as a Conservative, which they knew he wouldn't. So they put up a candidate against him: he was so upset by it. He was treated poorly. He was obviously a very good man, no question about that, an honest straight guy. It was unfortunate for him to be in that situation.

When he lost his seat, he took up the Show for two or three years, not very long, because he was getting on by then.

Charlie Boyce, right, the oldest member of Pilton WMC,
with Aunt Ede and Jim Govier

The 1980s

The Hardacre's daughter Pauline and husband Tony Sherwood became licensees at the Crown, taking over from Marj on 14th February 1989, the same day the Hardacres took over in 1950

George and Ronda de Gex happy in all-too-brief retirement

Stanley Williams' painting of 'Gathering Mangolds'

1980s *Pilton welcomed more 'incomers' as well as bidding farewell to some before their time. Margaret Thatcher's Britain was in full swing, Capitalism ruled and a new Tory MP for the Wells constituency, David Heathcoat-Amory, was elected in 1983 on the retirement of Robert Boscawen. The family came to live in Pilton at Beales House. Pilton was important for all three main parties in 1997, when Michael Eavis stood for Labour, while Philip was working hard for the Liberals. Nonetheless, Heathcoat-Amory continued as MP until 2010.*

A nationwide property boom was under way: houses had increased in value tenfold since the previous decade. Not all 'incomers' arrived in search of the best schools, others sought different ideals. Maureen Tofts, wife of now-retired vet Steve, friend to all animals, describes finding her roots:

In 1979 the Tofts family, Steve, Maureen, Helen 6, Jonathan 4 and Ben the Labrador were looking for a new home to try out a small slice of *The Good Life.* Eventually, during the week before Christmas 1979 we went to see a house in Pilton, unoccupied for nearly two years, with an acre of orchard. The executors of Miss Loach's will (the fifth owner) had not been given planning permission to erect houses on the orchard.

On a freezing cold day, two days before Christmas, we found our way to Bakery Lane. Trying to see the house was trickier than we expected, as the drive was blocked by overgrown laurel, so we had to cut our way in with a knife. There it was, the house of our dreams. It might have been in need of updating but it was love at first sight; you just had to see beyond the obvious problems. What if there wasn't a roof over the hall and you could see the clouds, and when you flushed the upstairs toilet the water went through the sides of the porcelain, through the floorboards and onto the ground floor? It was no big deal that you could pull at the plant roots that had grown through the wall plaster and watch the shrubs move outside. OK, so we couldn't get a mortgage for it but we knew we had to have it. It stretched us, and it hurt, but we managed to buy it by paying more than the asking price. Having parted with £40,500 we moved in at the end of February 1980.

So we hammered and painted, had village craftsmen help us to repair and build and like Topsy, the house has grown. It has seen the children grow up and leave home and welcomed grandchildren, Wiltshire Horn sheep and provided, what at times has seemed to be, quite a feast of hens for local foxes. Now I provide respite holiday care for my friend's hens (with no guarantee that they all return home).

During a winter evening, soon after moving in we were discussing house names. "Ahh," says Steve, "there is a magnificent ash tree in the middle of the orchard, what about calling it Ashfield?" So Ashfield it became: a shame the tree he was referring to turned out to be a walnut (it was winter).

Olive Linsley

Our neighbours were Olive and Jim Linsley. They had married in 1942, Olive having lived in Pilton all her life. Jim sadly died in October 1984 so we didn't have many years to get to know him. Olive quickly became a new Granny to our children. Olive adored cats (and cats adored her). Olive had a very cat-friendly lap and she could often be found in her favourite chair next to her Rayburn. Her cat food was always more desirable than the type we provided for our cats. She could often be seen tending Hope Cottage's pretty cottage garden.

In recent years I have had time to research my family history. All has fallen into place. Although I was born and brought up in Surrey, not leaving until my early 20s, I have been surprised to find that Somerset is my home. On my father's side I am directly related to the Sims, a farming family from Shepton Montague. An uncle, a few times removed, Charles Sims (died 1907) is buried in Pilton Churchyard. He was a tax collector for Pilton. I am also directly related to two local farming families, Dunkerton and Creed. Ann Sims (nee Dunkerton) my great-great-grandmother, was the main dairymaid for the famous West Pennard Cheese. This was made for Queen Victoria in June 1839. It was made with the milk of 737 local cows, measured 37″ diameter, 22″ high, weighed 10 cwt. and was carved in

Hope Cottage where Olive Linsley lived

mahogany, with oak and laurel leaves and the Royal Coat of Arms.

So here we are, only the sixth owners of this house that was built around 1818. We were meant to live here, and I have found my roots.

In the very hard winter of 1981/82, Rob Kearle recalls extreme snow:
We used to walk down the valley from Elm Farm as kids to collect eggs at Burford in the chicken sheds. I remember in the really cold winter of '80 or '81 when we had all the snow, we cycled along the back lane from the top of Whitstone Hill to Burford. We cycled over snowdrifts taller than the tops of the hedges. It froze over the snow and it wasn't until the snow melted that we saw cars had been

abandoned there, so we'd been cycling over the tops of cars in the drifts! The snow didn't go until early May on the north side of some of the hedges that year.

Shortly after my mother died in 1982, an odd thing happened, that John Fletcher turned into a short slot on Radio 4's series, 'A View From My Window,' as 'The Strange Case of the Policemen's Trousers,' although technically he'd have had to have an elastic neck or eyes that saw backwards:

Major-General de Gex used to live next door to me, in the house where Jenny still lives. I remember watching him from my window as he mowed his immaculate lawn, marching back and forth precisely and smartly as any guardsman on a parade ground.

But then one day something very peculiar happened. As he was mowing beneath his wall by the Pylle Road, suddenly he came across 28 pairs of abandoned policemen's trousers. Presumably thrown over there by some desperate miscreant fleeing the scene of a dreadful crime.

John Fletcher, not wearing police-men's trousers, with lurcher Flash

The constabulary were summoned, but could cast no light upon this strange occurrence. No one the General spoke to admitted to knowing anything about it. Everyone in the pub was perplexed.

So being a charitable man, he offered them to the needy. Myself, always being of a somewhat unkempt appearance, was offered them first. But pretty soon about half the people you met in the village were wearing policemens' trousers. They had a long special pocket in them in which to carry a truncheon. Ray Loxton reputedly used his to conceal eels in.

The General continued his immaculate lawn-mowing, back and forth across his bowling green lawn, but never again did he find a single pair of policeman's trousers. I have my own theories on this. It was at about this time that policemen on bikes were replaced by policemen in panda cars. Could this in any way be connected to this sudden mass loss of trousers? Were our policemen lurking in cars because they feared to reveal the long leg of the law?

Jenny writes: I also had a pair until they wore out: lots of buttons, no zip, so that may be why they were rejected! Although my father survived being parachuted into Arnhem and the Normandy Beaches, a hip replacement operation went wrong, so, far too young, aged 75, he left Pilton for ever in 1986. It is a strange irony that I have been able to enjoy their retirement home for far longer than they could.

The late Bob Scanlon and family moved here in 1983, leaving ten years later and writes of a 'Question That Changed Our Lives:'

The doorbell rings and there stands a lady who introduces herself as a neighbour; "How do you do?" I say and call my wife, Audrey to the door to meet our new neighbour. "Do you like jazz?" we're asked. "Yes." "Well, there's a big jazz festival here in the Summer." "Oh, that's nice." Then a surprising change of subject, "You have two white pipes coming out of your side wall." "Yes," I say, "they are overflow pipes." "Ah, *one* of them is, the other one is a camera Mr ***** (our predecessor) put in to spy on me." "*Really?*" "Yes and he climbed on to the roof of my house with a gun." This we found hard to imagine, since when we met Mr ***** he was having some difficulty even walking! "You must come round for coffee some time," our new friend invites and off she goes.

What sort of place have we moved to? We had just taken early retirement and moved to Pilton from Essex to start our 'Third Age.' It had all started well, another neighbour from across the lane had welcomed us with tea when we arrived and another couple had held the keys ready for us. But we had already had to call in a locksmith to deal with a key jammed in its lock!

Our fears were groundless – OK we had one weird neighbour, but we soon found that the people of Pilton were a friendly lot, even if some of them were 'characters.' Another kind lady appeared to say how welcome we were and, in conversation, she asked if we were interested in amateur dramatics. This was the question (or rather our answer) that changed our lives!

"Well," we said, "we'd like to find out more about it but we would only want to be backstage." So we bought tickets for the next Pilton Players production and were introduced to the place where, although we didn't know it at the time, we were going to spend many happy hours – Pilton Parish Hall.

Later we were invited to a Pilton Players production planning meeting and joined in with some play reading. Despite my earlier insistence that I didn't intend treading the boards, they took a chance and cast me as Mr Pearce in *Between Mouthfuls*. Not only did I tread the boards but had to travel with the Players to perform the play in the Somerset Festival of One-Act Plays. The play was set in a restaurant and the same food kept being served at each performance: it was pretty high by the end.

To my surprise, I enjoyed the experience and was ready for more. So started our life-changing 'Third Age' and the start of friendships that have lasted nearly 30 years. Audrey helped backstage but she also did some acting and took part in Festivals. I did some writing for the Players and a little bit of directing. We had found our niche.

People started to recognise us from our Thespian appearances and asked us to get involved in other village activities – like Pilton Day (as it was called then), Parish Council and the Local History Group.

I was encouraged to enter something in the Flower Show, so I tried my hand at growing from seed – not terribly successfully – my carrots showed a lovely top about 2″ across but only a ¼″ deep on top of a root about 18″ long and less than 1/8″ wide; the willow twigs I used as row markers sprouted beautifully but the seed rows they marked did nothing! Audrey had more success in the handicraft section with knitting – the photo shows her 'Long House' jumper knitted from her own design.

The Pilton stream ran through our garden, one day it suddenly turned a nasty colour, very cloudy and the trout and all the other water creatures were dying in numbers. I found that workmen repairing an upstream bridge had somehow allowed large quantities of mortar into the water. We were devastated at the loss of the fish but some months later the Environment Agency restocked the stream with young fish. It was fascinating to look on as they returned later to count the fish, stunning them with electricity.

One of the characters I mentioned earlier lived on the other side of the lane from us and liked to keep chickens, rabbits and so on. He bought a horse for his children but, lacking a stable, raised his garage door and attempted to keep the horse in with a length of rope strung across the opening. Predictably the horse escaped and found its way up to the main road. Fortunately someone managed to get it into a field before anything worse happened.

Regrettably, family and the need for a smaller garden took us away from Pilton but we have fond memories and, of course, we come and see Pilton Players in action whenever we can.

The 'Long House' jersey designed and made by Audrey Scanlon

Philip Eavis relates how this decade was an important one for the Liberals:
In 1984, the County Council elections were planned and the Liberals based themselves in the former empty offices left by Consumer Buyers. The Liberals won for the first time in 100 years.

After the County Council, there was the European Election, that was for Somerset and North Devon. It was the first time Liberals have won a European seat, all run from there. I was the agent and Chairman of the whole thing. That was Graham Watson and he's still there today; his campaign was run from there. He had been David Steel's PA.

Another Pilton Players stalwart, John Boucher, remembers productions from the '80s, as well as other local events:
We moved to the village in 1978. Woodfield Cottage was then a small, two-up-two-down cottage with a long front garden, into which I immediately planted countless untried vegetables. We were part of the happy hippy generation, moving out of the city to begin rural domestic bliss, and to begin with all went well.

So too did my early forays into village life. Like the over-enthusiastic vegetable planting, joining village organisations was carried to extremes. I was in Pilton Players, on the Parish Council, Flower Show secretary at Pilton Day and so on. Jane was left to bring up the children while I attended committee meetings. Life on the Parish Council in the 1980s and 1990s was particularly lively and time-consuming, with the Festival giving rise to endless meetings and strongly-held, divergent views within the village. From organising a Village Poll on the Festival, to advising the Council on a variety of legal matters including the creation of the low-cost housing on Top Street, via a number of contentious planning applications, life as a parish councillor was never dull. But not as exciting perhaps as trying to neatly park (for West Pennard School PTA fundraising) the anti-Thatcher Peace Convoy at an early Festival, and very nearly being squashed in the process.

During the second half of Her Majesty's reign, life became even more bizarre when I was persuaded to play the part of the Dame in a number of village pantos, many would say with monotonous regularity – and wooden acting. It was a case of always the Dame, and never the Queen (although I doubt whether Helen Mirren ever felt threatened, it would have been nice to have been asked...). I felt a certain affinity to Her Majesty, partly in the way in which we were both performing roles, also in the endless question of what to wear for the next public appearance: should it be the tiara, or (in my case) the silver wig? My wardrobe was slightly less extensive than the Queen's, particularly when it came to blue outfits, but I always felt my purples were far more eye-catching!

It has all been great fun, probably more for me than for Pilton Players' audiences, or those listening to me drone on at Council meetings. And, I have a feeling, rather more fun than having to be happy and glorious all the time. Being a real trouper, Her Majesty goes on and on; long may she continue to reign over us!

John Boucher in his silver wig as 'Gorgeous Gordon' and Sandra Howe as 'Wicked Wanda' for a Pilton Players' 1989 production of 'Mother Goose' written by John Howe

Pilton Players had something to say about incomers, as John Howe, author of many Pantos, depicted in a classic 'Jack and Bill' script:

INTRODUCTION

Jack and Bill in their incarnations as John Howe & Margaret Miles, John Howe & Margaret Windsor, John Howe & Liz Elkin must now be centurions plus. Very loosely based on characters from the village pub and the Working Men's Club, secure in their old ways of life, they struggled with a changing world of which they were highly sceptical. Their most scathing comments were reserved for the gentry and the vicar ("He be useless – never comes round to see 'ee 'cept when he thinks there's a cup o' tea in the offin' – but give him his due, he's damned good when yer dying!") Only 'they incomers' were more deserving of their scorn!

SCRIPT

Bill. Mornin' Jack.

Jack. Mornin' Bill.

Bill Hasn't seen 'ee for a fair few weeks. Thought per'aps ee'd gone on down the churchyard – you know sort of permanent like.

Jack. No chance of that. They'm so packed in down there b'aint no room left for an honest body. Mind t'aint so warm upon that new burial ground – the wind from Glastonbury do fair whistle up there. Ah! If 'ee was to 'ave yer ashes a sprinkled there, why you would end up as that there atomic fallout over Evercreech.

Bill. I don't think I should fancy that!

Jack. Don't suppose they at Evercreech 'ud be too keen either.

Bill. Still we mustn't sit 'ere a getting all mortified – we got a lot to be thankful about.

91

Jack. Yes. I'm glad that Geoffrey Howe raised the threshold for Capital Gains tax. T'will help to cancel out the tuppence the blighter's put on our cider.

Bill. You don't suppose Geoffrey Howe be related to that new lot what's moved in down opposite the church do 'ee?

Jack. Shouldn't have thought so. 'Less of course 'e's the black sheep of the family.

Bill. Wot? That teacher chap?

Jack. No that danged Chancellor.

Bill. Maggie Thatcher ain't no better. "No 'U' turn", she says. But she's going clean round the bend like *Harpic*!

Jack. More like *Domestos* – her do kill 99% of all known firms!

Bill. Still, they do still give us a few shows and circuses to take our mind off things.

Jack. Aah! The Royal Wedding went off lovely and t'weren't a bad party up at the Hall. I enjoyed they sausage rolls but I weren't too sure about they *vol au vents* mind.

Bill. Ah – I looked 'em up in the French Dictionary when I got home. It do mean 'flying with the wind.'

Jack. Ah! That do seem about right – I'd thought t'were the radishes!

Bill. They 'ad a dance after. Still don't suppose 'twas like the dances we 'ad in the old days out the Bush.

Jack. No. Dancin's always bin – wot my Polly do call one of my little foibles.

Bill. Ah! You've always been knowed round 'ere for yer little foibles

Jack. True! I'm proud to say that over the years I do reckon to have exercised 'em more than most.

Bill. Yes, you'm infamous for it.

Jack. Do 'ee remember the song us used to sing about 'em?

Bill. 'appen I do.

Jack.. Whatever were it called then?

Bill. Us didn't dare call it 'foibles' right out like.

Jack. No – 'twere "Our Funny Little Ways"

Our Funny Little Ways
To the tune of the Lincolnshire Poacher

When we were young in Pilton, boys – 'bout sixty years ago
'Twere in the Roaring Twenties when the skirts were short you know.
The girls was all called flappers then and a Charlestoning would go
Yes! 'Twas our delight on a Friday night to let our foibles show
The Forties brought us World War Two – our duty was quite clear
To rally to the flag, my boys and save our country dear.

We delved and dug for victory wi' they land girls down Steanbow
And for King and Queen and country, boys.
They helped our foibles grow.

The Festival of Britain – it were held in fifty one
We took a coach to London – saw the Skylon and had fun.
The Big Dipper down at Battersea it excited us you know
And then in the Dome of Discovery our foibles were best in show.

In the Sixties I went training to be an astronaut
To make the first moon landing it was my cherished thought.
The gaffer 'e did tell we – friction makes re-entry slow
So t'was our delight in orbital flight to see our foibles glow!

In the Seventies, we got with it, lads – joined the ranks of Hippydom
I learnt to sing they protest songs – on my guitar I did strum.
I decked myself with beads and flowers and with garlands hanging low.
Why! We covered ourselves in forget-me-nots so our foibles wouldn't show.

Now we're into the Eighties, boys, and we be getting on
We've lived through nigh a century an' still we're goin' strong.
With age we've come to Wisdom, lads so now we do understand
That it weren't ours but others' foibles what has muggled up this land!

Jack. I'm a bit worried, Bill. Some of them Pilton Watch Committee do claim we have *double entendres* and hidden dirty meanings in some of our songs.
Bill. Well, I'm danged. T'would be a surprise if anyone could find any meaning in 'em at all.
Jack. Bain't a lot of meaning nor sense in anything these days. Tiz all topsy turvy. There's a lot o'they new 'ouses bein' put up in the village – all h'equipped with h'every modern convenience.
Bill. I do 'ear that a lot of 'em do have they bidet things.
Jack. An' very 'andy too when yer getting on. Tiz easier to do your feet in one o' they rather than stand on one leg with yer foot in the sink!
Bill. Nary a one o' they new 'ouses 'as got a privy.
Jack. Makes 'ee wonder where 'em do go for a smoke an' a good long think. Sides where do the baker leave the bread? Do 'ee mind when we had to carry the Elsan bucket down to the end of the garden by the stream?
Bill. Ah, but they eels were never better.
Jack. Rabhaulin's gone right out of fashion. Nowadays, t'ain't eels and mash – tiz they scanty an' chips.

Bill. Don't get many o' they for a quid. They're fashionable tho. Everythin's about fashion an' bein' trendy these days. Most o' they newcomers only live out 'ere a long wi' we in the country so as they can pretend they're country folk – playin' at bein' landowners. We got a song about their pretensions. Tiz called –

In a Pilton village garden
To music 'In an English Country Garden'

Now, it's the fashion to keep a flock o' woolly sheep
In a Pilton village garden
When 'e've finished all your chores it's so good to get out doors
In yer Pilton Village garden.
Lambing very late at night
Worming when the time is right
Tears when 'e gets to eat the family pet
You're a budding Bo Peep
With a flock of Jacob's sheep
In a Pilton village garden.

Oh, they Kings did arrive with about a dozen hives
For their Pilton Village Garden
We be filled with wild alarms
When the little devils swarms
In our Pilton village gardens.
That queen she is a buzzy bee
The workers busy as can be
Flying long hours to pollinate our flowers.
When they return to their hive
They do a little jive
In a Pilton village garden.

Every person we do know seems to 'ave a dog or so
To guard that Pilton village garden.
They barks and they bite, keep'n us all awake at night
Ne'er an owner begs yer pardon
Man's best friend is running riot
Ne'er a moment's peace and quiet.
Break the sanitary rules with
Their little piles and pools.
The only remedy is to raise the licence fee
And save our Pilton village gardens.

Oh, they newcomers indeed, do arrive with fancy seed
For their Pilton Village gardens.
The old sorts we adore – they totally ignore
In their trendy Pilton gardens.
Courgettes by the ton they grow
H'artichokes in h'endless row
Garlic and herbs, even aubergines they sow
They pigeons I declare
Dine on continental fare
In their Pilton Village gardens.

Now each lady and gent hold a fund raising event
Advertised in *Homes and Gardens*
On a balmy summer's eve
Your purse they will relieve
In their Pilton village garden.
Munch your cheese and sup your wine
On strawberries and cream you dine.
You'll get bitten by the gnats
And dive bombed by the bats.
The gale force north east breeze
Makes your cups of coffee freeze
In a Pilton village garden.

A couple or two have built a barbecue
In their Pilton village garden
It takes Dad half the night to get the thing alight
In a Pilton village garden.
Chicken kebabs they prepare
Steaks that's nearer raw than rare
Charcoal and coke fill the air with acrid smoke
Then by twelve or thereabouts, Dad can't put the damned thing out
In his Pilton village garden!

Jack. Reckon it be time fer me mug o' cocoa.
Bill. Yes, tiz time I sent my Lily upstairs to warm up a spot fer I.
Jack. Which spot be that then?
Both. Good night, folk.

They both hurry off.

The Princesses competition to celebrate the 1981 Royal Wedding

The Royal Wedding in 1981 of Prince Charles and Lady Diana Spencer inspired a fancy dress 'Princesses' competition, as shown here. Fairy tales don't always have happy endings. Prince Andrew, Duke of York came with Fergie to Pilton as a private guest to the 1988 wedding of the Wootton's daughter, whom he had known at Gordonstoun, to the son of then Defence Minister, George Younger. But to the best of our knowledge, Diana never visited, although Prince Charles officially opened the new houses at Oathills in June 2010, also checking out the Festival, of which more later.

It was still a carefree time for children growing up – cycle races down Bread Street, organised pancake races such as the Pancake Olympics.

Candace recalls the freedoms of childhood and her son Joe's young Eavis friends:

It was a lovely place to bring up Joe: trust and safety were so different then. It was great for Joe to have Emily and Ben. They'd all been at primary school together, then Ben to Whitstone and Joe to the Blue, then the Cathedral School because of Emily. They've stayed such firm friends, which is so good.

Joe Fletcher and Emily Eavis playing in Festival mud in 1985

In the '80s and '90s, Ebenezer Chapel was featured in several magazines as an example of a colourful, quirky, creative artist's home:
The room at the Chapel was a framework on which you could elaborate. It was a place you could exhibit. The stencilling along the ceiling and wainscoting has now totally been painted over, which is so sad. I repainted the wording, the Methodist mottos and like to think created a special space. So why, when I sold, would someone buy something with all that history and obliterate it all?

Candace was mainly working on tapestries and needlepoint in the '80s, but an interest in mosaics, for which she is now best known, began when: with Joe, I went down to the stream that I now live beside, where he'd play and we'd find little blue and white shards of china. Just by the bridge, by the weir. We collected enough to come back to the Chapel and he was sort of windowsill height at that point, so he must have been about six. We mosaiced a windowsill and that was the beginning of my mosaic work. When you dug in the garden then, you always found blue and white china. Now you find very little. I remember that so fondly, getting a little heap together.

In his book, Douglas Turner describes how:
Judith came into farming in the '80s after visiting Australia. She rang me up from Australia, where she and Clive were travelling in 1985 and asked if she could come home farming and I said 'Come on straightaway.' I was delighted that Perridge was going to be a family farm passed down the generations, just as Gwen and I always planned it should be.

Farming has changed a lot since I was a boy. If we ploughed one acre per day with horses we thought we were doing really well. Now you can plough ten acres a day with a tractor.

Douglas Turner (R) in the mid-60s in front of Perridge House, with Judith to his right and Shannon beside her

Rob Kearle began working at Worthy in the mid '80s:
I used to work for Dennis Clapp who had Cockmill Farm, with all the Festival site land over the river from Michael's. So the Jazz Field, the Green Fields, King's Meadow, where the Stone Circle is now. I used to work as a Saturday and holiday boy. Then he died so they decided to sell the farm, on one condition, Michael could only buy the farm if he took me on. So I was sold into slavery with a neighbouring farm!

Michael sold Jon Thorner the farmhouse and a few acres because in those days he needed to repay bank loans.

So the first time I met Michael, I was weeding the garden down at Cockmill. He used to stutter quite a bit then. "You'd best come over to the farm, then." I had to go and sit in the kitchen and have a cup of tea with Jean and agree to work for him. If he didn't take me on, they wouldn't sell him the farm!

Andrew Kerr recalls how, once the first Glastonbury Festival (for CND) began in 1981:

Having helped on the farm, I did odd jobs around the village, such as stone walling, and became festival site manager by default.

Josie Hiscox had a few cows in the buildings at the top of Cockmill Lane. I milked them and took a 10 gallon churn on the back of a tractor to Dennis Clapp's farm down the hill and tipped it into his bulk tank, he usually helped. One Saturday, he didn't appear but this youth with spikey hair and a tartan apron came out, with a broad grin on his face. That was my introduction to William Burroughs. Bill was later to design and build the current Pyramid Stage, replacing the former one burned down in 1994.

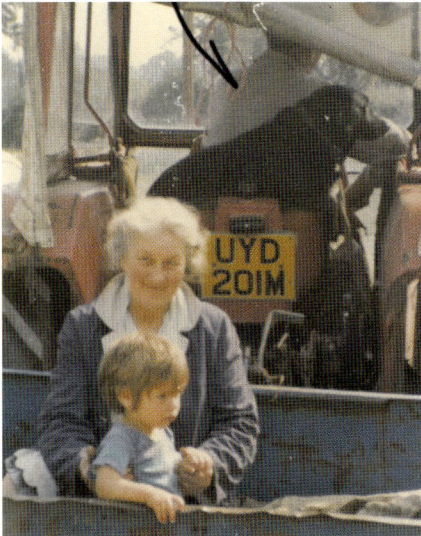

Josie Hiscox and Joe Fletcher

Josie Hiscox with donkey Friday by the Village Hall, with (left to right) Gus Rodgers, Luke Thomas, Carol Taylor and Demelza Thomas

Knitwear designer Annie Fewlass was a Piltonian for a year or so, before moving to Shepton. She remembers Josie Hiscox' donkey, Friday, who somehow managed to herald Pilton's 'rush hour' with great precision, twice a day, morning and evening, even though that consisted of only three cars! You could tell from his braying....

Not everything was rural or idyllic: the Festival was increasing in size each year, since its revival in 1981, attracting a rougher element, what some called the 'drugs and thugs era.' Tony Bailey recalls how this affected his strawberry growing:

Jimmy Milne was going to help. We got the horticultural chap for the South West to come out. He told me he didn't think I'd be able to grow strawberries at Culverwell because it was too stony and too wet, claggy soil. But I grew some brilliant crops there. In the spring, the stones would help the soil warm up quicker. He thought it would be prone to frost. But we did it for about 25 years from 1965 the first crop to 1992, the last.

When it started, we had gates, simple posts with barbed wire across. They used to throw their coats over the top, tip themselves over so they didn't get caught in the wire, and go down and help themselves to our strawberries. We had fun galore. So then I started picking some when the Festivals were on and taking them down there and selling them from the back of the pick-up.

In 1980 or '81 I bought Copse Hill from Harold Butt and started growing them out there. We had fun and games over a lot of Festivals but not to start with, as initially it was families camping there. I always associate it with the 'drugs and thugs era' from the mid-80s. Before that they'd be playing football, no problems at all.

1987 was the worst. There was a load of Travellers camped up in the corner of Butts' field next to us. Two young girls were camped in a small tent nearer us and they came back to find the tent trashed and all their belongings chucked over in our long grass area. They reckoned it must have been the Travellers. They hadn't been out of there two minutes when a van came crashing through the barbed wire fence, heading straight for our strawberries and I realised that Kath was down there picking.

Then they turned around, crashed through the next fence into Butts' field, heading off towards Graham Bailey's bungalow. For some reason they headed towards the hedge that runs along the Bridleway and I seen them get out of the front, open the back, pour petrol on it and next thing it went WHOOSSHH! I ran across and called to Graham & Doreen to get them to ring the Fire Brigade.

That particular year I had friends from Avalon (Chemicals, later part of ICI) with pickaxe handles to keep them out. You only had to turn your back for two minutes and they were in there pinching strawberries.

That lovely old ash tree, the skeleton's still there now, is actually regrowing. We used to put all the strawberries under there when picked. One lunch time, they went up there and cut all the branches off, obviously for firewood. I had an old gate that Ray Norman gave me that I was going to put in the Bridleway but they took that and burned it. That was those Travellers, because I found the hinges in their fire, after the Festival.

We phoned the police and CND "Oh, we're coming," but no-one came. They were scared, having found vans full of weapons. "We can't come in case we cause a riot."

There was a Canadian there, I turfed him out three or four times. On the Sunday afternoon I was getting a bit worried when he said "Oh, I haven't killed anyone in a long time." They were in one of those VW vans. So a friend and his mates came down and they disappeared once they knew we had back-up.

Afterwards we couldn't pick the six or eight rows nearest the fence around the fields. We sprayed *Jeyes Fluid* right to the top of Copse Hill. I saw what I thought was this discarded sleeping bag, so I sprayed right over it. When I got up to it, two heads popped out!

Kath Bailey picking strawberries

Tony Bailey and Rotavator

Campers too close to the strawberry fields. Note the orange VW van: this was the Canadian's

In his letter to the Shepton Journal, printed on 2nd July 1987, Tony wrote summarising these tales of woe, saying :
I have lived in Pilton all my life and have a respect for other people's freedom which has helped me keep an open mind, over the years, towards the festivals. But I must now say enough is enough.....

Such incursions into the village were commonplace at that time, and on site, oversized Rastas with axes or chainsaws attacking hedges were not to be meddled with. Michael promised to get on top of drugs and crime problems and eventually allowed police on site. The Parish Council held a referendum in September 1987, Mendip Council took a Poll later that month: all of this is in the Village History Society press archives. If we tell this story in detail, there would be no space for anything else but we couldn't resist including the odd anecdote, in this case from Robert House, electrician on the Festival site since the early days:
For a while 'Dub' tents were all the rage, then one year instead of a tent the crew arrived with a complete pre-fab house, which was duly assembled and ready to go, except the door was upside down and the doorstep was two feet high. Another year a group demanded free electricity and things got a bit heated when I said "no." They weren't that bad though, a few weeks after the Festival they were on TV preparing to run from Land's End to John O'Groats for charity.

One year there was a huge Afro Caribbean guy armed with a machete sharpening sticks. I could hear Michael Caine saying, "Don't throw those bloody spears at me!" Eventually curiosity got the better of me and I cautiously approached the man and asked what he was doing. "Roots, mon," was the reply. I said, "What?" "Roots – sugar cane, mon." My spear maker was splitting sugar cane ready to eat and he gave me some.

The upshot was that it became a ritual dance every year, with last minute granting of the Licence, prosecutions, fines for breaching the licence. Topsy grew and grew, officially 55,000 in 1987, a year in which police found an alarming haul of weapons. The event began distributing funds locally to West Pennard School and PTA, Pilton organisations such as the Youth Club, Playgroup, Football Club, Playing Fields, Carnival Clubs and Rotary in exchange for stewarding. This practice has since expanded to include other neighbouring schools or charities, as festival numbers have tripled. In 1989, although a Festival featuring more theatre was on the Licence application, Mendip asked for numbers reduction to 40,000. More attended as it became a music event with Van Morrison topping the bill. Mendip Council attempted to keep tighter control and it was the first year there was a fence, lower than today's, to try and keep people out. No chance!

In contrast, at the Bath & West Show, Pilton Women's Institute showed off their fine work. Margaret Drew remembers:
Between 1979 and 1997 Pilton WI entered the group competitions held in the Marquee on the Village Green at the Bath & West Show. Each entry had to stand in an area no larger than 2′ 10″ wide, 2′ 2″ deep and 3′ high. Each year we were given a title to illustrate. This had to include three individual crafts by three different members, the display and design could be by any number of people. In 1978, having visited the tent where these entries were on display, I reported to the WI that I thought the overall standard of work was very poor. The President at that time was the Hon. Mrs Fraser, who immediately threw out the challenge to do better! Unable to resist, three like-minded ladies started something which, for us, became a lifelong friendship, for Pilton WI put us in the spotlight for several years.

The Sailor's Return

Valerie Schofield, Sue Boon and Margaret Drew became the three to beat. That first competition was *A Fairy Story* and we eventually made *The Little Match Girl.* Between the three, we had many craft skills: wood carving, fine sewing and canvas work were the crafts used that first year. The greatest fun was making all the small items to set the background scene. We won first prize with 495 out of 500 points.

Over the following years we were severely tested but managed to win many times and learned when lost. More members joined over the years: some stayed with us, like Rita Ayres, Wendy Lynn, others not so long.

Our exhibits often had to be protected in the Show by ropes to keep poking

The Little Match Girl made by Pilton WI

fingers out! The greatest unintentional praise came from a disgruntled competitor of another WI branch: she said it was so unfair that Pilton won all the time, "after all, they are professionals – they work for Harrods." It just happened that our morning coffee flask and tools for setting up were in an old Harrods carrier bag!

Each year after the Show, we set up the exhibit again and had a coffee evening for village friends to have a closer look. We tried to be accurate with details, for example, when the sailor's uniform was made, Commander Fairley was consulted about badges. After that, he would call in for a weekly report! It was rewarding to stand back and listen to onlookers recognising things from the past that we had contrived in miniature: the model figures helped bring these scenes to life.

A total of 15 challenges were met by Margaret Drew and her team between the years 1979 and 1997: themes included D Day, Children's Books, Showtime and Celebrations. The crafts included sewing, needlepoint, wood carving, model figures, appliqué, Dorset buttons, and soft toys.

Many lasting friendships were made whilst talking and working on the many and varied projects, to say nothing of the tea and biscuits consumed well into the night.

In the mid-80s, Sheelagh and John Allen's son, Rodney, then only 16, started playing local gigs as a singer and guitarist, often playing at the Club as well as other local venues, including the Festival.

Rodney Allen plays guitar on a visit to the Blue School to film a video to go with the title track of his first album 'Happy Sad'

The English love a chance to dress up, as Sandra Howe describes:
Sometime in the 1980s the Working Men's Club advertised a Fancy Dress dance on a Saturday night. A group of us planned to go. I was dressed as the Queen of Hearts and my husband chose to be a Fallen Angel! He borrowed one of my nighties and the costume was completed with the addition of a wonky halo, a copy of *Playboy,* an empty gin bottle and an enormous pair of sparkling wings last used by the Angel Gabriel in the school Nativity Play. Invited to drinks in Bread Street before the dance started, the wings were left at home. When it was time to leave, the rest of us walked on up the hill to the Club and the Fallen Angel collected his wings from our cottage. They were easier to wear than carry, so they were clipped on and he hurried out into Shop Lane and followed us up the hill past the church. Before he reached the corner, a car, headlights blazing, came down Shop Lane and the angel was illuminated in all his glory against the backdrop of the church tower.

The angel, of course, could not resist flapping the gigantic wings! They were golden and must have looked very eerie caught in the car headlights! The car screeched to a halt, did a U turn with horn blasting and sped back up Shop Lane with the driver obviously frightened out of his wits. We are not sure what happened when he reached the main road and wonder what he told his family when he reached home!

That would be perfectly normal at the Festival these days, where theatre groups from all over the world dress exotically and stalls sell fairy wings and fancy dress for all ages and sizes.

Pilton Players brought home a prize, in a claim to fame or a case of 'David and Goliath,' as John and Sandra Howe recall:
In the 1980s, Jim Major, much experienced in Somerset Drama circles, joined Pilton Players. Silver-tongued, he quickly persuaded us that we had talent and he, the directing ability, to enter the Somerset Fellowship of Drama competitions without losing face. Over the years and many certificates, cups and shields later, we reached our crowning year in 1988. We entered the One Act Play competition presenting Jimmy Chinn's *A Respectable Funeral.* Sheila Steward, Valerie Schofield, Sandra Howe and Bob Scanlon played three sisters and a brother meeting in their mother's run-down house after her funeral. It was a play of pathos, bitterness and finally, tenderness. The cast grew into the parts – starting in Somerton, then the County Final in West Monkton, the Divisional Final in Swindon and the Grand Final for the whole of the western side of England at the Playhouse Theatre in Weston-super-Mare. We had made the big time – the All England Final at the Grand Theatre, Lancaster. WOW**!**

Elation quickly gave way to despair. Only 15 members and just £9 in the bank! John sat at the end of a phone for a day raising sponsorships from local firms. Jim's neighbour provided a minibus for the cast and drove it. *Living Homes* provided a van for scenery and props – over 260 individual items – and Martin Steward drove that. Came the hour our new kitten, Poppy, saw us off on the Friday evening from the Hall car park. A tedious, fretful journey up the M5 and M6. Seedy Morecambe didn't exactly resemble its more glamorous counterpart, Blackpool. The burnt out pier looked out on the sullen sea, its skeletal remains catching those lights along the Prom that were still working.

'Theatrical digs for strolling players' we had joked on the journey trying to keep our spirits up. Oh, dear! What had John booked for us? Rooms in five Edwardian houses unhappily joined together and full of people rather the worse for wear celebrating in advance the next day's family wedding! Along a dimly lit corridor, scruffy carpet and more doors than you would expect. Sheila and Martin, John and I shared a room – well almost! A fibreboard wall split the original room and the one bay window. When Martin put up his window, our half went up too! How we laughed and then felt we should really only talk in whispers. We didn't sleep much and were pacing up and down the Prom before 6am; met the others, thought of Eric and Ernie and rehearsed the words of the play 'wot Jimmy Chinn had wrote!'

The Grand Theatre, Lancaster was an 18th century building that had once been grand but was still imposing for a 15-strong village drama group. Down and down we went into a mirror-lined dressing room in the bowels of the theatre

Pilton Players' winning production 'A Respectable Funeral' by Jimmy Chinn with Val Schofield, Sandra Howe and Sheila Steward

– fusty and smelling of mould. Never mind! It had been good enough for Ken Dodd and Les Dawson. 'How tickled we were!'

We were *David!* The groups from Welwyn Garden City and Skelmersdale might each have been G*oliath* with 750 and 300 members apiece. Many of their actors were ex-professionals keeping their hand in. We had two supporters in the audience. One, 'Ric Schofield, had been 'persuaded' by his wife Val to watch her act for the first time. The nerves jangled, the theatre was huge, and the audience measured in hundreds not our usual dozens. The other plays were greeted with rapturous applause from a partisan audience who cheerfully ignored a confusion of acting conventions. Our play was met with a studied lack of response. The judge announced the winner – not us but the locals. We bit back our disappointment and took on board the judge's comments which patronizingly praised an 'inexperienced' group in a 'small' play. Were we disappointed? Yes! But we did realise that it was the experience of a lifetime. Out of the blue, Rowntrees of York wrote us a generous cheque for our expenses. A long drive through the night after a Mayoral reception in the Town Hall. Arrived in Pilton at 4.30am. Poppy, in the car park, alternately miaowing and purring. Good to know you've been missed!

From 1988 the vineyard was under new ownership, so the village welcomed Anne and Jim Dowling, who writes:
In the autumn of 1986 when we were living in Surrey, I told Anne that I would like to have a go at making English wine. Naturally she didn't think I was serious, but fate took a hand. Shortly after our discussion she visited her dentist. While she was in the waiting room she picked up an unusually up-to-date copy of *Country Life,* and spotted an advertisement for an English vineyard at Pilton. Pilton also happened to be near where Anne's parents had moved from their home in Scotland.

We completed the purchase of the Manor House in December 1986 and moved in February 1988. Most of my working life up until then had been spent in the computer business, so this was an opportunity to do something very different.

Jim and Anne Dowling and David Heathcoat-Amory MP at the new winery 1989

I knew almost nothing about growing grapes and making wine, except owning a vineyard was widely regarded as a sure-fire way of making a small fortune, provided you started off with a large one. Fortunately, Pilton Manor Vineyard had two assets. The site, by English standards, was ideal. The other was Steve Brooksbank. He knew how to grow grapes and how to make good wine. He also trained Steve Melluish who became an invaluable and essential part of the winemaking team. There was also a third advantage in coming to Pilton, which became apparent over time and that was the village community.

Knowing how to produce good wine is essential, but as far as the authorities are concerned the most important job is collecting the tax. About half of the money brought in is paid back to HM Customs and Excise. Making a profit from producing wine anywhere is difficult, particularly so here in England. But it has many compensations: you don't need to travel very far to work and it's very satisfying and fulfilling to be involved in the whole process of winemaking. You can also drink and enjoy the results – in moderation!

John Avery, of Avery's of Bristol, was very supportive to English winegrowers in general and to us in particular. John's advice to us in the art of blending wines, was key to our later success in producing award-winning wines.

The current owners of the Manor no longer have vines or vineyard.

In 1988, Cynthia Mitchell retired as postmistress; the front shop had doubled up as the butcher's. Newcomers, Robin and Sally McLean, soon settled in, minus butcher's block, and Robin became Treasurer of Pilton Show for the next ten years.

In 1988, Michael Eavis announced his intention to give some of his land above Top Street for

Cynthia Mitchell and the old butcher's block

affordable housing, which took a while to go through all stages of the planning process. It was "a departure from the village's structure plan" according to Mendip's then planning chief. But it worked.

In June 1989, SAVE Britain's Heritage became involved in trying to save the Tithe Barn, one of only 6,000 Grade 1 Listed buildings in the country, in suggesting that planning applications be refused for development around the site of the Barn, covenanted never to be used for the Festival, which remains the case. Application was in for two new houses by interim owners, developers from Bristol. This changed in 1995 when Michael Eavis bought the land and Barn and set up a charitable Trust in 1996 for the purpose of restoring and caring for the building.

In 1989, Rachel Govier became Shepton Carnival Queen, the first of Jim and Eileen's daughters to be crowned. Sarah was Queen in 1990. The tradition continued with grand-daughters Megan, Rachel's daughter, in 2009 and Chantelle, Gary's daughter, in 2011.

In September 1989, the Rural Life Museum in Glastonbury showed the paintings of self-taught primitive painter, Stanley Williams, then in his 80th year. There were four brothers, of whom only one now survives, living

Rachel Govier as Carnival Queen 1989

Sarah Govier as Carnival Queen 1990

near the family farm at Cockmill. Stanley's paintings of rural life show changing farming traditions, painted in an unsentimental way. They are a record of a vanished world, where the horse has been overtaken by mechanisation.

'Gathering Mangolds.' Mangold wurzels were grown as animal fodder

Some might think there is too much about Pilton Players in this chapter. Panto chorus, everyone, "OH NO THERE ISN'T!"

The 1990s

Anne Goode and the cross made of telegraph poles that she installed on her land in the 1980s. Many services have been held here and it is floodlit at night. In 2011 it was replaced and rededicated by Anne's daughter Vivien

Michael Eavis and dandelion clock, with the original Pyramid Stage behind

1990 was the year of the Poll Tax riots but this discontent failed to reach Pilton, except at the Festival, in a year of major unrest and disturbance, mainly caused by Travellers already moved on here from Stonehenge by the police. This year was particularly bad and Michael recalls that:

The Convoy years were hard. That was really tough. They called themselves the Peace Convoy but they were anything but peaceful. It culminated in 1990 because the Magistrates said, "You've got to accommodate the Peace Convoy. Can you take them off the roads of Somerset and just put them somewhere?" So they had to come, you see, that was the Magistrates' ruling. On the whole, they were good-humoured and we've always been great on the humour front, the Eavises, we've always laughed a lot. There's just a problem with their culture, the violence, deaths and drugs and things.

Since the Magistrates said so, I gave them a field the other side of the farm, they had their own stage and everything. It worked for a while, for about five years. Then there were too many of them and too many of us. With the riot I thought this was the end. However, that big riot meant I had the police on board from then on.

In those days, Melvin Benn (later to become the Festival's Licensee from 2002-2012) was working on the gates with the Workers' Beer Company. He phoned me from Gate Two, saying "Michael, they're coming over." "What do you mean, coming over, they've got buses, they can't go through banks and hedges?" He said, "Quick, quick, we've got a real problem." So I shot down in the red Land Rover and said, "Look what are you trying to do, we've made a place for you. Follow me, follow the red Land Rover." Leading the way, I drove all up Springfield and along East Compton. They thought I was leading them up the garden path, so they all hooted their horns and stopped. I said "What's going on?" "Oh, you're just taking us away, we don't believe you." A little girl, about 12, said, " But that's Michael Eavis." They said, "*Is it?* That's all right, then." So they got back into their cars and buses and I took them all round by East Pennard and down to the top of the Cockmill fields we had.

Afterwards, though, they went on the rampage and armed gangs attempted to surround the farmhouse and the Police HQ at Benleigh. They also attacked properties in the Cockmill valley. Jon Thorner wrote to the papers some months later explaining in graphic detail : "what really happened to a few people caught up in this huge money-making peace-shattering event held in the depths of some idyllic countryside."

Robert House and his team of electricians were on site. He describes what was later named the Battle of Yeoman's Bridge:

Nathan and I were pulling out electrics from the bottom Market area after the Festival in 1990. All day an ex-army lorry had been driving round over piles of rubbish – bound to end in damage or injury. Three Land Rovers of 'Security' arrived and stopped the lorry, something was thrown, I don't know what, and there was some shouting. Suddenly from a gateway ran a shouting group of about 50 people, they captured two Land Rovers, setting fire to one, then a group split away running up the hill toward the farmhouse. I rang the farm, Jean answered the phone, I told her there was trouble and to lock the doors. Michael came to the phone and I gave him a running commentary.

A night of wanton theft and destruction followed. Hired generators and cables were either smashed or stolen. It was a demonstration of the fragility of 'Civilisation.'

Back in the village, Jenny de Gex remembers:
Returning home on the Monday evening of the Festival weekend, after an evening in a peaceful neighbouring village, to find police helicopters with piercing searchlights hovering directly overhead and plenty of noise and mayhem: like something out of a film, I thought, *here in Pilton?* Can't be true, I thought, must be dreaming. But it was no dream and continued most of that night.

There comes a point when anarchy cannot continue unchecked, so this episode proved a turning point for controlling future Festivals. Previous security 'guards' had been somewhat reckless or unreliable, almost as much a liability as those they were hired to control. Vulnerable properties from then on had their own security guards, provided by the Festival. Some were young, with little idea where they were; others were older, with resulting consequences. Confusions still arose, as Jim Cellan Jones relates:
We had a man called Wally, who I think was in his 80s, as our security man for a while. When there seemed to be trouble, suddenly he vanished like the snows of yesteryear. I remember once we had a group of people wanting to get into our garden and I was coming round the corner with an armful of beer cans, and I heard Maggie saying, "No, you're not coming into our garden." This man, who had a group with him, said, "Yes I ****ing well am." I appeared and said, "Shall I hit him with my bare fists or with these beer cans?" Fortunately there was a noise and a police car came round the corner. I called out "Officer!" The police came and said, "Now, sir, we don't want to go into the gentleman's garden, do we ?" "F...ing police." "No sir, leave, or would you prefer a nice ride in our car?" And off he went, on foot.

On a quieter, more sombre note, 1990 began with the sad and untimely death of Joan Bond of Burford. As her son Christopher wrote:

She was a very social person and during her time, had many parties, such as strawberry teas for Pilton children, led by Susan Green. Although she was born in India, where her father was in the Civil Service before Partition, she never lived there but her curry lunches were famous – guests breathed fire afterwards! She arranged for the then Bishop of Wells, later Archbishop of Canterbury, to meet Pilton Church members. He came to her funeral. She loved people: she was never happier than when introducing people to each other and had a very vibrant personality.

Sue Green and children at their holiday club at Burford, with Joan Bond

Joan Bond

Earlier in 1990, Candace Bahouth completed a heraldic tapestry for County Hall in Taunton, commissioned the year before to mark the Council's centenary. Later this decade, her first book, on needlepoint, was published; others followed, on mosaics.

In April 1990, Malcolm Fraser was High Sheriff of Somerset and among his many official duties that year, opened the new Visitor Centre at Glastonbury Abbey.

That same month, Anne Goode, speaking for the 'Friends of Pilton' formed to fight Council decisions concerning Festival licensing, spoke out, saying among other things: "British justice protects citizens from intimidation; it should not encourage it. This huge monster event will be rolling by its own momentum and nothing anybody can do will have any effect on anything." *On the other side, supporters said it was a charitable event raising considerable amounts for various charities. This disparity of Goode versus Eavis rumbled on for most of the '90s.*

In the summer of 1990, excavations were under way, managed by Birmingham University Field Archaeology Unit, on a site just off the Fosse Way outside Shepton Mallet, where large lorry parks and distribution centres are now. Early one Sunday morning, a distraught Fay Weldon appeared on the doorstep, saying, "We've got to stop them, they're going to concrete the site over. They've just uncovered a Roman cemetery, a burial site, whole skeletons lying in open graves: tall men, local soldiery, no doubt. We can't treat the dead with such disrespect. How can we get publicity?" *To which my reply was,* "If you can't get the press on board then no-one can. Here's the phone, let's phone the BBC Newsroom in Bristol." *That evening, film crews were on site and the resulting publicity succeeded in* "buying extra time to get the excavations put on hold, local church groups to sit around the open graves in that very hot summer to make sure further excavation was indeed halted, and for the Bishop of Taunton (the Bishop of Bath and Wells declined – the unearthed skeletons had presumably been pagan) to come with his crook and conduct a fitting ceremony over the remains of the dead – some of them possibly the forebears of those still living in the area today," *according to Fay. The finding of a Christian Chi Ro amulet in one of the graves had suggested at least some of the dead weren't 'pagans,' and also generated national interest. Truth can indeed be stranger than fiction.*

Newcomers moved to Totterdown, bringing an international flavour with them. Trinidad-born Grant Goldie, after Oxford University and a spell back in the Caribbean, came to work for EMI in Wells in 1973, and house hunting brought him to Totterdown Farm. He viewed the landscape in a different way, particularly apt in this Olympic year:

15th December 1989. A pretty ordinary day really, with post lying on the carpet. Usual stuff, bills, credit card statement, but one envelope was unfamiliar, thus the first to be ripped open. "Congratulations, Mr Goldie. You have been awarded a place in the 1990 London Marathon." OMG! What was I thinking, when I idly decided that it would be fun to enter this famous race, as I watched the 1989 London Marathon from the comfort of my armchair.

I experienced a mixture of excitement and panic. Here was I, nearly 49 years of age, who hated long distance running with a passion. I loved cricket, soccer, sprinting, long jump, squash but road running was always avoided at school, even feigning illness if necessary.

I told myself to be sensible. I was too old, unfit and had only four months to train for the toughest of all races but would this opportunity ever arise again? I needed advice from an expert and a work colleague of mine, Bernie Mundy, who had run several 'Londons,' confirmed all my fears, emphasizing that "at your age you need at least a year to prepare for a marathon."

I was unmoved, as the London Marathon had now found its way onto my bucket list. Bernie saw my resolve and agreed to help only if I promised (had there been a Bible handy I would have been forced to swear on it!) to follow his training schedule to the letter. I was committing to training six days a week (no respite on Christmas Day) over the worst of the winter months. My first run would be five minutes (nearly killed me) and my last would be three and a half hours. My objective was simple – to complete the course without walking and live to tell the tale!

And so my adventure began. Home from work, into my running gear, up the hill on Totterdown Lane and then backwards and forwards *ad infinitum* across the road above my house. Always in the dark, often in the rain (sometimes even in snow) or fighting the wind and fearing for my life, as I ran under the bending boughs of trees and listened to the noises of the night. At first I would take a torch but that was soon abandoned as my eyes grew accustomed to the moonlight. How I loved the full moon and the freedom it gave me.

Even better were weekends and my long runs in the daylight. Every lane around Pilton became my friend. I discovered the beauty of Pilton and the surrounding villages as I searched for new routes to keep me motivated. Adventures abounded. Whether it was the flock of aggressive geese at North Wootton or the various dogs who took an interest in my exertions. Some more than others, like the two Alsatians frantically chased by their concerned owner as they headed from the disused rail track straight for their prey as I approached the dump at Croscombe. The local farmers soon came to recognize me, none more so than Eddie Masters who gave me an excuse to pause for a chat before wending my way again between the herds of cows.

Friends and family were abandoned during these months, except when they were asked to contribute to CLIC, my chosen charity for which I was to raise £1,000 pounds thanks to their generosity.

Finally the big day arrived. I assembled at Greenwich with the other 30,000 aspirants not knowing what to expect. 4 hours 22 minutes later I had achieved both my objectives. I had finished the London Marathon and had run all the way. My life had been changed forever. One more London Marathon, 20 Half Marathons, several 10 km and 5 km runs: I had become a runner.

Sally Goldie describes her Pilton years:
I arrived at Totterdown Farm in Pilton in April 1991 and Grant and I were married in June 1992 in Pilton Church.

It was not long after this that Totty Milne invited me to help with the Flower Show, first of all collecting up and cleaning the many lovely cups (with Eileen Whatford's help) and then becoming more and more involved over the years.

Sally Goldie enjoying an English country garden

Being Australian, I always celebrated Australia Day on 26th January and this continued when I moved to Pilton, having earlier lived in Portugal. Captain Cook did the right thing by discovering Australia in January when it was hot! For us in the Northern Hemisphere, every year was different and some years we had snow, others it was icy, or heavy frost or just plain freezing! But it was always a fun evening for those 20 with Australian connections. Everyone had to come dressed as an Australian and over the years, from memory, we had Crocodile Dundee, Dame Edna, a surfer carrying a surfboard and Australian cricketers.

Another memory we have of Totterdown Farm was allowing the Jesters Carnival Club to build their float in our big shed. This involved months and months of hard work and it was always a great thrill seeing it heading off down the lane to join the other Carnival floats in Bridgwater.

Now that I live back in Australia, I have fond memories of the badgers coming through our garden and eating the apples on the ground, the deer eating my roses, the hedges, the blackberries, my hanging baskets, and the beautiful views we had towards Glastonbury and the Tor.

Two weeks after celebrating their 40th wedding anniversary in 1990, Douglas Turner's Australian wife, Gwen, died. He continued to be involved with the local farming community, the NFU up to Executive level, and the Rural District Council.

In 1991, Finn Christensen purchased Steanbow Farm which he had farmed as tenant farmer since 1973. He was Chairman of the NFU South West Regional Advisory Board and has since developed Steanbow into the large successful business it is today.

On one memorable occasion, I drew the curtains here to find the garden full of cows. Thinking they were from Worthy, gone walkabout, I called Steve Kearle,

Finn Christensen and family at Steanbow, April 1997

even though it was only 7.30am. He came round and said they were Finn's, so between us all, we herded some 40 cattle out of the garden, down Hitchin Hill, not before they had happily munched and trampled everything within sight! The NFU paid up more promptly than I have ever experienced with an insurance claim before or since!

In 1991, John Fletcher won the Giles Cooper award for a radio play for a drama written for the BBC, 'Death and the Tango.'

1991 was a year off for the Festival, to consider future tactics: the new main charity would no longer be CND but Greenpeace. The other main village event, Pilton Show in September was lucky enough to have a free aerobatics display by a member of the British Aerobatic Team. A month or so before the show, I noticed an amazing, heart-stopping aerial display over Pilton and started a newspaper campaign 'Who is the mystery pilot?' which helped the Show publicity. He turned out to be Anne Goode's stepson, just waggling his wings on the way home from a Show elsewhere. So he agreed to do the same on the afternoon of the Show, which fortunately was fine enough to do a dramatic daredevil display.

In 1993 Pilton Parish Rooms celebrated their Centenary in several ways, one being the publication of a booklet of 100 years in historic photographs. In 1890 a meeting was held to form the Pilton Working Men's Club. In memory of his late wife, Edmund Clerk of Burford offered to rebuild and restore the whole building, then in considerable disrepair.

'Aunt Ede' Hiscox, in Victorian fancy dress to celebrate the centenary of the Parish Rooms and Club which her grandfather helped build in 1893

This became the Village Hall, the original library room became the Club, the WI met upstairs, the Happy Circle at the back, Pilton Players held performances there, all manner of events took place, and the Youth Club met in the cellar. Increasingly running out of space, the 2000s decade saw changes fulfilled but meetings and discussions rumbled on throughout the '90s.

Edith Hiscox, then Pilton's oldest resident, joined others for a Victorian Evening to celebrate the Centenary.

Ashley Robertson, Edith Hiscox's great-nephew, affectionately remembers times spent with one of the village's more colourful characters:

I have many great memories of Auntie and some of the most vivid are from many years ago, when my brother and I were still in short trousers. We loved visiting Auntie: her house was like Aladdin's cave, full of old and interesting things to explore and marvel at, like her prize figurines, lots of old paintings and best of all the red and gold glass fishing floats that hung from the ceiling. We would twist and spin them and watch the colourful streaks of light flash around the room.

We would also eagerly await the pocket money Auntie would give us so we could venture over the hill to visit Mrs Strickland's shop. The shop's big red door always seemed to need a little nudge to get it open, and after it had shaken the bell into action, Mrs Strickland would appear from somewhere beyond to supply us with black jacks and fruit salads, which we happily chewed on the way back to Auntie's.

I also remember Auntie taking us on many Sunday School outings to far off places like Swanage and Bournemouth. It was always a great day out; we would have fish and chips for lunch and ice creams on the beach for dessert; happy days.

Auntie was like a second mother to us and she always said she didn't mind not having children of her own, as all her nieces and nephews, great nieces and great nephews were her children; she certainly loved us all as if we were her own.

Auntie's other great love was living in Pilton. She was a valuable member of the community and she spent many years as a mainstay of the Pilton Players. I still chuckle at the memory of Auntie dressed as the grey friar in one of the star productions. She also seemed to be forever the organist at the Methodist Chapel, playing well into her nineties: she may have missed the odd note now and again but she certainly made up for it with passion and commitment. I still miss Auntie, she really was what family and village life is all about.

'Aunt Ede' died in her 95th year in November 1998. The youngest of five children, she had lived in Pilton all her life. After she left school, she trained as a cheesemaker, working on nearby farms, cycling to work.

Liz Elkin relays a tale Ray Loxton told her:

Ray has always owned dogs and in 1993 he was walking with Spotty Dog in the fields at the top of Stoodley, when he disturbed two people in the grass. "I was still apologising for interrupting when blow me the dog had flushed out another pair further into the field. It was obvious that the two couples didn't know the other was there and I thought it best to walk on by. By the time me and Spot got to the other side of the field, we had intruded on three separate couples, each wearing less than the last! On the telly at the time *Lady Chatterley's Lover*, with that Sean Bean, was at its steamiest and I've always thought that was the cause of three in a day."

Ray Loxton

One pub regular, Cheech, had an unfortunate incident on his way back from the Crown one evening, as Liz Elkin relates:

If it hadn't been an away game the incident would probably never have occurred. Cheech always took his dog, Dixie, to play pool at the Crown and, as she had pale fur, she shone like a beacon, leading the way home. Dixie could not travel to away matches, so Cheech was walking from the Crown to Bread Street alone. When he crossed the bridge at the weir he tripped, the rail caught his thigh and Cheech toppled into the stream gashing his head on the jagged end of a water pipe.

He scrambled out of the stream and staggered home. When he caught sight of himself in the mirror he understood why his son had gone pale as he welcomed him home. The mix of water, mud and blood was not a pretty sight.

Cheech with Dixie

Although he was not in great pain Cheech realised the cut on his head required attention, so they travelled to the Accident and Emergency department in Bath. In 1995 junior doctors worked very long hours and despite his own dazed state, Cheech recognised that the doctor was at the end of a long shift. They decided it was best to let the next shift deal with the injury and 26 stitches later the wound was repaired and the patient was fine. The bridge at the weir and the incident acquired the title 'Cheech's Leap.'

Mike and Fiona Case took over the Long House and for a while ran it as a B&B, before splitting the house into two and selling land to build the New House (yes, another one....):

We are told that the Long House history extends back over 200 years. There must be many worthwhile stories associated with its long and prominent position. Lifetime villagers can probably add more, and these notes are of necessity second-hand, because some of the characters have left us, or perhaps do not wish to identify with the tales; some of what is told must be 'allegedly' so.

Becoming a hotel brought its own particular problems. When one lives in such surroundings, it is not difficult to see where John Cleese obtained his material for *Fawlty Towers*. Although not this particular establishment, numerous similarities presented themselves.

It was some time after we took over that we were told the tale of *The Ghost of the Long House.* Certainly it was never mentioned by the Estate Agent when we purchased the property. We need not have worried, in any case it is not a subject we take seriously. I was told that a relatively well-to-do lady had been staying as a guest, and had been experiencing visions of something white floating across the bedroom, and a disembodied hand scrabbling across the dressing table. It could not be explained, so the vicar was called for (whose son told us the story).

Whether the exorcism could be said to have worked or not is a matter of opinion, but an explanation was soon forthcoming. It seems the lady had a new personal maid, staying in the next room. Whether she was coming to check on her sleeping mistress is unclear: perhaps she had been crawling across the floor to avoid any disturbance? For whatever reason her hand was reaching upward into the lady's handbag. Her continued employment is unknown, but at least the ghost was laid.

Another two tales came to us via Olive Linsley, who lived opposite. On one occasion she was visited by a guest from the Long House, who said she had been waiting over half an hour for her pudding, and had seen no-one. On visiting the kitchen via the back door, the neighbour found the acting chef/waiter fast asleep in a chair next to the AGA cooker. She managed to rustle up a pudding for the lady, making some excuse. The matter was never again mentioned by either party!

On another occasion, noticing water running through the ceiling from the room above, the chef pressed the room intercom and shouted "Whatever you are doing, stop it!" Unfortunately he hit the wrong room button, and had contacted a very surprised honeymoon couple!

We had our own events to cope with: in the early days we provided various evening meals cooked by Fiona, with a choice of three puddings. On one occasion the favourite was meringues with cream and fresh raspberries, which most of our guests had chosen. What happened next ended with Fiona striding up Pylle Road almost in tears. When she retrieved the large tin of previously prepared meringues, she found it to be alarmingly empty. I managed to excuse the mistake and provided *Peach Melba* instead. Explanations came later when a shamefaced son admitted that he had thought they were cakes for the family, and devoured the lot.

A couple of years after we had started the business, there was a knock on the front door. I answered. "Hello Mike, how are things going?" I must have looked a little puzzled because the man continued, "I expect you remember us." His wife smiled sweetly, "How is Fiona?"

I would like to say the faces were familiar. Were these friends from our past, perhaps holiday acquaintances, or old work colleagues: no, they were almost total strangers, although there was a

Mike and Fiona Case at the Long House

certain distant mist of recognition. " You'd better come in. Have you travelled far? I daresay you would like a cup of tea." I had made my excuses. At that point I could hear Fiona approaching. Saved.

"Look, dear. Look who it is." Poor Fiona shared the same dilemma. I could sense her thinking, "Who the hell is this?" She covered well.

It was only after tea and a few probing questions that we found out that the couple had been two of our very first guests. Obviously the impression we had made on them was not reciprocated. In our defence we had probably catered for a couple of hundred other 'faces' in the meantime, and the early days were something of a blur. No harm done, they enjoyed their tea, and in fact returned as guests a couple of years later, none the wiser!

Not all events are humorous though, and probably our greatest dilemma came not long before we left the trade. Asleep in an upper room one night we heard a commotion in the dining room. The door to guest accommodation was always locked overnight, so we thought we had burglars. On reflection we would probably have preferred that. What we found was some of the contents of dining tables disarranged, sugar bowls upturned and on the floor. We also caught sight of a large rat scuttling into one corner. Chasing was fruitless, and the rat disappeared into an understair cupboard and up between the wall and the old loose plaster. Calamity. This rat unlike 'Basil' was not tame and we could not easily catch it. Guests were due down for breakfast in about four hours. Help! We quickly decided the dining room must be out of bounds. I must explain to the guests that they would need to have a tray breakfast in their rooms, the excuse being an undisclosed calamity in the dining room. I might have mentioned ceilings or something but the guests were quite happy. Fortunately all were leaving that day. All foodstuffs were destroyed, all china and cutlery thoroughly disinfected and washed. The dining room was closed for a week and disinfected, with guests being directed elsewhere. The rat was discovered and dealt with. It appeared he was not really a resident, but had entered through a slightly open ground-level window, which was then closed and permanently sealed.

Not an experience either of us would want to repeat, although in total running the Long House was enjoyable, though certainly not lucrative! One great thing is all the nice people we have met as a result of coming to live in Pilton. Many will remember Aunt Edie (Hiscox). On our 25th wedding anniversary I was called to 'the presence.' "I want to give you something," she said, and handed me a ten pound note. I protested. "You are a pensioner. You can't afford to do things like that." "**I am 90,**" she replied, "**I can do as I please.**" No answer to that! I have tried the same line, but it just doesn't wash when you are a mere 65 or 70!

Robert House describes how:
Part of the joy of on-site working, wherever, is the contact with others and so it was with Johnny Allen, snake wrangler!

Nathan and I were working at Bourne Farm. We looked out of an upstairs window to see Gandalf trying to persuade a 30 metre coil of perforated drainage pipe to sit properly in a drainage ditch. He would secure one end, start rolling the coil down the ditch and then the start of the pipe would flick up and start rolling towards him and begin to wrap itself around him like a boa constrictor. John would then start all over again.

Mike Lewis joined us, curious about our laughter. By now John was covered in a film of mud which had dried then cracked and looked like scales. He resembled an armadillo. Gandalf eventually wriggled free from the clutches of the anaconda and spotted us at the window and shouted, "Come on you **** give me a hand." It is difficult to take an armadillo seriously.

Ron Ballantine was Chairman of the Parish Council from 1993-2003, an unenviable task, as many major confrontations concerning Festival licensing and building and planning applications were all up in the air during this decade. His reminiscences follow:
Before I retired, I drove out of West Compton for the Unilever offices in Bristol at 7.00am each morning and got home after 7.00pm each night, and only experienced the Pilton area between Saturday morning and Sunday night.

So, following retirement, I set out to know more about our surroundings and soon got pressed into a vacancy on Pilton Parish Council. Some few weeks later, Bob Scanlon, the Chairman, retired and I got a phone call from Dick Skidmore saying that the Councillors were asking me to be Chairman. While not stated, this was clearly on the basis that no-one else wanted the role! Thus began ten years of a roller-coaster ride on the lowest tier of local authority. Our non-political Parish Council had little 'power,' and was mostly sandwiched between what the residents didn't like and the little that Mendip District Council (which we referred to simply as 'Mendip') allowed us to do.

When I joined the Council, a near neighbour, Charlie Boyce, had served on it for many years, as well as serving for periods as a District and County Councillor. His helpful guidance was invaluable. At that time, there were up to ten individual Boyces in tiny West Compton, in three related families. With the steady decline in farming locally, there are now none living in West Compton.

Perhaps I should describe a Parish Council meeting back then. The scene is the 100 year old Village Hall. Just inside the entrance door, on the right, is a room called 'the Library' because it reflects Edmund Clerk's intention to educate and divert the working men of Pilton. The room was damp, in poor repair, and heated (?) by an electric fire for the benefit of Councillors, crammed around the one table that fills the room, along with a metal filing cabinet where the Parish Clerk kept the Council's papers. When members of the public attended, additional metal chairs were un-stacked and squeezed into the corners and the atmosphere got even thicker.

On the first Monday of each month, Chairman Ron says "three minutes after 7.30 so we may as well start the meeting." At that, Jean Warry the Clerk cries "give me a couple of minutes to get my papers in order." Five minutes later the Chairman tries again. Then the door creaks open and Chris Frewin comes in. "I'm not late am I?" To support this view, Chris King then strides in behind him "Sorry, I had to finish some photocopying." John Boucher growls that it is important that we finish in time to go home and watch *Spooks* on TV. With all the Chris's now aboard the Bounty, Captain Ron sets sail hoping there will be no mutiny tonight.

The reason why Council meetings were held in the Library was that the WI had the Hall booked for its meetings on Monday night and we could not forego the rent! Some years after I became Chairman, we took the momentous decision to move our monthly meetings to Wednesday, when the Council could actually get use of the main hall. This meant meeting around trestle tables set up in the middle of the hall, with several rows of chairs laid out for the public. Very often we had three senior Pilton ladies ('the public!') attend and more than once we heard one of them say in a loud whisper, "This is much better than *The Vicar of Dibley* and at least it's (nearly) live!"

Every few years, the Charities Commission would confront the Parish Council because Councillors were also the Trustees of the Village Hall (which in 'charity asset' terms included the premises occupied by the Working Men's Club). They claimed we did not keep Parish and Charity matters sufficiently separate, were too cosy with the Club and did not charge it a proper 'market rent' for the use of the charity premises it occupied, despite the fact that the Club paid an annual contribution to the running of the premises. Thank goodness we had John Boucher as a councillor, as his legal expertise kept the Commissioners at bay for several years!

However, some aggressive lawyers at the Charities Commission office in Taunton finally had enough and issued threats to the Council which individual Councillors could no longer ignore. As proposals were already being developed for a re-designed building to replace the existing premises, the Council arranged for a new group of Trustees, which included representatives of all village organisations, the Working Men's Club and the Council, to take over the running of the Hall. Charity Commission attacks on the Council fell away, and the new Hall Trustees set off from strength to strength.

When we vacated the Library and moved to the Hall, the problem of what to do with the Council's filing cabinet arose. Jean Warry, the excellent Parish Clerk, proposed that it could be accommodated at her home where husband Paul had other papers stored, since he was Council's equally valuable Treasurer – and also treasurer of a number of other important village organisations. Little wonder Paul always came top of the poll in the four-yearly Council elections!

When I joined the Council, one of the problems it had to deal with was known as 'Cock and Bull Drove.' It seemed that the Caravan Club had issued a five-caravan certificate for a field on the edge of Pilton, without Mendip raising any objection. Following complaints from local residents, the Parish Council took up the matter with the owner of the field and Mendip, both of whom so successfully batted back all the issues we raised that Cock and Bull Drove was still on the agenda as I left in 2003.

Other items that appeared on the agenda month after month included a proposed (but never achieved) footpath on the main A361 between Top Street and the phone box, the problem of where Ray Loxton, our gravedigger, was dumping the earth from new graves, and the 'simple' matter of putting up road names on parish roads. On the last, following discussion with residents, Chris King reported some five preferred names for the road from Pilton to West Compton ranging from Totterdown Lane, to Burford Lane, to Summers Hill Lane! Council left the final decision to Mendip! I am sure that Sandra Howe still has some of these items on her agendas.

Obviously, the biggest matter the Council dealt with each year was the Festival. On the basis that the Council tried to represent the whole range of village opinion

– from those wanting the Festival to be stopped altogether to those who thought it the best thing that happened in Pilton – Council concentrated on trying to reduce as much as possible the nuisance to residents. In earlier years this included the Traveller convoys, the noise, the vehicle movements, and the ticket-less hordes rampaging through village gardens looking for the next breach in the wire fence. For years our efforts had only limited success, while the numbers licenced to attend rose from around 70,000 to nearly three times that number today. Mendip and the Police each viewed their efforts at control quite satisfactory, while the Parish Council sat between them and dozens of complaining residents who insisted otherwise. Some of my worst evenings were spent chairing special post-festival meetings of irate residents with representatives of the Police and Mendip. Others were those when phoned up at 2.00am to be asked if I would just get the b****y noise to stop at once!

Real improvement only came when the Mean Fiddler organisation took over the management of the Festival and brought in the professional experience they had gained elsewhere. They seemed to understand that the key to most of the problems was to concentrate on the fence, making it strong, non-scalable, tunnel-proof and well guarded. Over a few years, this meant the number of ticket-less festival-goers arriving in Pilton reduced and control improved. I believe also that the Parish Council today has better communication with the management and the event itself has changed in nature.

The lasting reminiscence I have from my time on Parish Council was just how much labour Councillors put in, on top of attending monthly meetings. As well as dealing with the Charity Commissioners, John Boucher spent hours making sure that Council's views were accepted when Trusts were established for Gabriel's Orchard and the Tithe Barn. Chris King travelled the Parish's footpaths and made sure they were some of the best in the County. As well as being contact with the Youth Club, Fiona Case and husband Mike ran a Village Contact point at the Long House during the Festival. Chris Frewin provided expertise when planning issues came up, while Dick Skidmore and Robert Kearle (although rarely in tandem!) could be relied upon to tackle most problems in the village. And I've already highlighted the input of Paul and Jean Warry to the Council and to other organisations.

This leads me to reflect that it is the people involved that are important, not the institution itself. In retrospect, I appreciate the good times we had.

In 1994, plans for low-cost housing of ten houses at Oathills were approved and these were built and completed in 1995.

Also in 1994 the original Pyramid Stage was burned down, following an electrical fault, in June, just weeks before the Festival. Instead a temporary orbital stage (used by Pavarotti in London!) was used that year, followed by planning application for one of the more unusual cowsheds – you've guessed, pyramid shaped! Bill Burroughs from Steanbow made a model which Michael accepted and we still see today.

Firemen at the Pyramid Stage June 1994 after a 'horrendous' fire

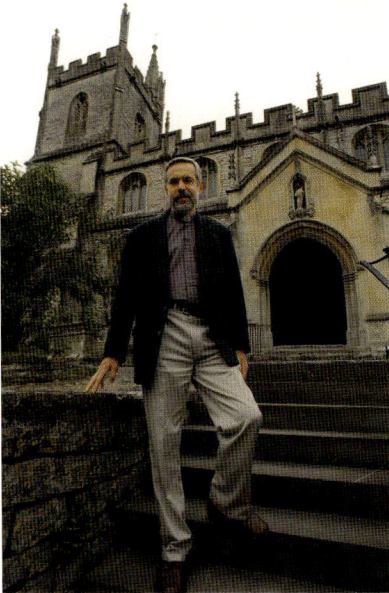

The Rev David Osborne arrived as Rector of Pilton in 1994 and has been here ever since

In August 1994, a new vicar, David Osborne was welcomed at a service in the village church led by 'Bishop Jim' Thompson, then Bishop of Bath & Wells. With hindsight, David writes:

It was October 1993 and there was an advert in the *Church Times* that interested me. Four parishes in Somerset were looking for a Rector. I had been the Rector of four parishes in Shropshire for nine years and wanted a move, ideally to the South West.

So I looked them up on the map and sent off for more information. It said that the population of Pilton was 1,000 people, but 100,000 during what it quaintly called 'the pop festival.' Four parishes and a festival. I applied and was shortlisted.

Sue Green was on the interview panel, together with Bill Bartlett, Keith Armstrong and Graham Chambers; with Dick Acworth in the chair. They decided they wanted me to come and we moved in July 1994 after Tom had finished his GCSEs. He would go to Strode College and Ellie would transfer to Whitstone.

Nearly 20 years later, they have moved on, and in church life many things have changed. In the church building we have carried out repairs and alterations. Eva Krebs had been a mainstay of the church for many years. A remarkable woman who had left Eastern Germany with her parents to escape persecution in the 1930s, she had ended up as a local nurse, living in Pilton. When she died she left her house to the church and with the proceeds we were able to build the new vestry and toilet and install good facilities for catering and flowers.

The bells have been re-hung and increased from six to eight. We improved the heating so that the church is now comfortable, even in winter, and makes an ideal venue for concerts and other performances. We have re-wired the church and installed new lighting, carried out regular repairs, and responded to thefts of lead, furniture and the chandelier. Now we are about to repair the inside of the roof and treat it for woodworm.

Within the community there has also been both continuity and change. Anthony Austin was churchwarden when I came and is now doing another stint. Gill Eavis also did two stretches. Paul Warry has done over ten years, and Anne Dowling and Maurice Davies have also served as churchwarden.

Other folk have joined us. Some have moved in; others have been born here and we have been able to welcome them with baptism. Others have left; some moving away and others dying. And all the time I have been here I have worked together with Sue Green, a Reader who does an enormous amount for the church and the community.

There is a concern among bishops that a lot of clergy are isolated: having a lonely time working away on their own. That has never been my experience here. I have always felt part of a team. When things have been good, there have been other people to enjoy them with; and when they have been tough, I have had support.

When I lived in the Midlands or the North I often had a feeling when I drove past Bristol that I was coming home. It was strange. I had lived for a couple of years in West Somerset and spent a lot of time in Devon and Cornwall. But there was no specific place. From my first week here, from my welcome service and a couple of evenings later when Jim Govier bought me and Madron a drink in the Club, there was. Pilton was home.

David, now a Prebendary and Sub-Dean of Wells Cathedral, is Rector of Pilton with Croscombe, North Wootton and Dinder, and also a member of the Iona Community, a published author ('A Country Vicar,' 2004) and poet, and a leading light of the village Green Group.

In 1995, stalwart of the village, Charlie Boyce, passed away.

In 1996, Candace Bahouth had her first large solo exhibition at the American Museum in Bath. It proved highly popular and had record attendance figures.

1997 was a happy year for Doug and Ivy Fleming, who celebrated their Diamond Wedding Anniversary. They received a card from the Queen, mentioning that she and Philip celebrated their own Diamond Anniversary that same year.

The seeds were sown for Music in Pilton in 1997, as founder Sheila Steward remembers:

Sometime in 1997, David Osborne, Rector of Pilton, was talking about the Church building and wishing that more people could see it, use it, perhaps make music or produce plays in it. This was thought to be a good thing, so a small group formed, calling itself *Music in Pilton* and set about presenting concerts. The aims were to have a variety of good quality performances, to pay fees to the musicians, to be non profit-making and to keep ticket prices as low as possible. Since Millfield Brass gave the first concert on 6th June 1998, 25 concerts have delighted us with jazz, opera choruses, mixed choirs, male voice choirs, the Vicar's Choral from Wells, sopranos, baritones, children from Wells Cathedral School, brass soloists, Celtic harps, guitars, penny whistles, organ solos, woodwind, piano quartets and string quartets. All the musicians have commented how satisfying it is to make music in beautiful surroundings.

Music of a different kind down the valley had one of the worst muddy years, as evidenced by these photos by Ian Sumner, for which no captions are needed.

In the General Election of 1997, Michael Eavis stood for Wells for Labour but the Tories held the seat, by a margin of only 528 votes. The Liberals' campaigns for both Wells and Somerton and Frome were run from Pilton, as Philip, Michael's brother, was then agent for both constituencies, chairing the campaign team.

The major event of that year however was the sudden death in a Paris car crash of Princess Diana, with a resulting tidal wave of emotion such as this country had never seen before. This unfortunately coincided with the week of the Pilton Show, as Philip Eavis, then Show Chairman, recalls:

We had to cancel the Flower Show – the heart of the Show – but people got together in a spirit of solidarity afterwards. There would have been no stewards, no entries because everyone was watching the funeral on television. It was a difficult decision to make. She died on a Saturday night and we didn't think for one moment the funeral would be so soon, as there was so much contention about everything. Then the Royal Family announced it was to be the following Saturday. We already had our marquee up, tables, chairs, toilets, so it wasn't a question of losing deposits, we would have lost total costs.

Robin McLean, then Treasurer, worked out what our losses were going to be, we had no reserves at that time but we have done ever since. We went to the Playing Field and he went to George for the Legion, asking if they were able to pay thousands of pounds which of course they couldn't possibly do. George Windsor, a wise, sensible, pragmatic man said, surely the solution is to cancel the Flower Show but continue to use the space otherwise. Here we have a quiet gentle man coming up with solving a crisis. The following year we made him President of the Show, he really worked hard to the end.

George Windsor by the marquee on the Playing Fields for Pilton Day

Philip sent out a letter to everyone in the village, detailing the plans for the weekend, saying how "the organisers have considered many factors, some of them concerning the Princess herself. She was a person who devoted a great deal of her energy and time to supporting good causes" and for that reason, there was a collection at the Friday night Party towards Save the Children's work bringing relief to those injured by landmines and campaigning for their abolition.

No one appeared on the field until about 3.30 pm after the whole extraordinary event and outpouring of national grief had unfolded on TV screens. It was almost as if it was a relief to be with people again, although there was the mood and atmosphere of a wake.

In 1997, George Windsor was given Life Membership of the British Legion and awarded one of their highest awards, the National Council's Gold Badge, at a 50th anniversary supper of the Pilton Branch held at the Club.

In 1998, Gabriel's Orchard became a reality and not just a dream, as Joe King describes :

Jim Dowling, at the Manor, was inspired to set up Pilton's Community Orchard, on some of their land. Once the initial planting had been done it was time to take stock of the situation. We were keen that as many people as possible would be involved with the Orchard and offered all the trees for sponsorship. Quickly, virtually all the trees were sponsored and Pilton's very own calligrapher

George and Margaret Windsor dressed up for a special 1940s evening at the Crown

Malcolm Drake designed a handsome certificate, presented to all the sponsors, identifying the variety of tree, and a map showing exactly where the tree was in the Orchard. We were very keen to identify trees locally that had been significant to Pilton, and were very lucky in having the assistance of Liz Copas, apple expert, who joined us visiting a number of the old local orchards, where she identified apple varieties. Richard Raynsford mapped the trees and their positions in the Orchard. We were again very lucky in discovering Les Davies, former Showering's Apple Officer, who taught us how to both bud and graft the varieties which we wanted to preserve, and how to prune as well. Together we grafted approximately 90 young trees on M25 rootstocks. These grew on for a year in the Manor's vegetable garden and then some were planted out in Gabriel's Orchard. We were also able to offer a number of the young trees to the owners of orchards from which the grafts had come.

The trees grew on for a number of years. It is not considered good practice to encourage them to fruit heavily in their early years but eventually we reached the moment when we had sufficient fruit to consider producing our own Pilton apple juice. The Pilton Show Committee generously gave us a grant to purchase equipment to make juicing possible, and Philip and Gill Eavis kindly provided us with a site to work from. In the first year we produced 250 bottles, some single variety and some blends. In our second year we plucked up the courage to enter

our juice in the appropriate classes at the Royal Bath and West Show and won first prize in the Community Orchard apple juice section. As the amount of crop slowly increased, we decided to branch out into cider production. We were very grateful for the assistance of Neil McDonald of *Orchard Pig* for his advice. Our first year's production of 210 litres was a very good clear cider, which was very dry. Hopefully our next batch will be a little sweeter.

Our activities have caused media interest in both television and newspapers. We also regularly get contacted by other fledgling projects wanting advice about how to proceed.

Usually we have a working party on the morning of the first Saturday in most months. Everyone is welcome to come, it is a light-hearted affair with plenty of chat and refreshments. Any of the Managing Trustees will be delighted to give you information and directions, currently these are Chairman Richard Raynsford, Treasurer Jim Dowling, Secretary Joe King, plus Martin Steward, Robin Cade, Christine Davies, and Christine Nicholson.

The first pressing in 2000 of apples for cider, gathered from Gabriel's Orchard

Margaret Miles writes 'Funnily Enough' about her late husband, John:
I was married to John Miles for 43 years before he died in February 1998. I had known him for barely three months before I married him, so I think it's true to say I didn't know much about him. One thing I knew, because his parents had told me, was that as soon as he could hold a pencil he could draw. And on

our wedding day his father took me aside to give me a sound piece of advice, "You'll have to manage the money, because John doesn't know the meaning of the word!" Truer words have never been spoken! John would rather give away a painting or drawing than charge for it.

He drew cartoons from a very early age, then, after National Service, he worked in Clarks' art department and then for May and Baker at Dagenham. An art department in a more exotic place followed: Bermuda, where he also drew a political cartoon every week for the *Bermuda Sun*. During this time he drew many more cartoons, selling them to *She* magazine, *Woman*, *Woman's Realm*, *The Daily Mirror* and others. Back in England from 1967, he drew a kind of psychedelic cover for *Punch*. This was when we were living in Horningsham and John was working on the murals for Lord Weymouth, the present Lord Bath. He worked in the Kama Sutra room and all I can say is, he enjoyed his work immensely!

His cartoon strip *Perkins* was created shortly after we left Bermuda, when we were living like hippies on the island of Hydra, off Greece. But it wasn't until later, at Horningsham, that it was picked up by an agent for syndication in America and the rest of the world. It was a captionless cartoon and ran in a great many newspapers. Under the name of *Cicero*, it was the first cartoon strip to be published by the *Sunday Times*. On the agent's advice, the name changed to *Perkins* and as such, ran for some time in the *Daily Express*.

In about 1970 we came back to Pilton to live. John continued to draw the strips and contribute cartoons to other publications, as well as painting portraits, designing typefaces, Christmas cards, working on a series of abstract paintings and, as if that wasn't enough, writing poetry!

Every year since we married, he drew a Valentine's card for me but in 1998 my card was only half finished, he'd still been drawing it the night before he died. Funnily enough, it's the one I treasure most.

One of John Miles' original sketches for the syndicated cartoon 'Perkins'

Sketches by John Miles on his funeral service sheet

130

Maureen Tofts writes of Tom Harris, bell ringer:

Tom was a real gentleman. He lived on Whitstone Hill all his life. Born in the 1920s, he joined the church choir and, as was often the case, once his voice broke he was sent upstairs to learn to ring the church bells. He had served in WW2 with the Black Watch (Royal Highlanders). He never spoke about his time in the war and it remains a mystery as to why a young man from Somerset served in a Scottish Regiment. When we rang half muffled for Remembrance Sunday, a haunting sound, he could sometimes be caught with a tear in his eye.

Tom Harris

Many of the current village ringers remember Tom, all with great affection. He passed on some strong values, the importance of ringing for Sunday service, helping other towers when they are short of ringers, valuing everyone's contribution to the tower's ringing, regardless of their ability, and maintaining the tradition of ringing the bells. These values are the ones Pilton ringers still hold dear today.

In 1956 Tom had seen the bells lowered down the tower to be overhauled and hauled back up with new bearings and repaired wheels. He was unbelievably enthusiastic when, in 1996, the six Pilton bells were sent away to be overhauled, returning in fine fettle and joined, soon after, with two new bells to make it a ring of eight in time for the Millennium.

Tom always had a quiet word of encouragement for us. Even today he is fondly remembered for the amazing pained look on his face when we rang poorly, which we often did (and indeed still do). At the end of the touch (about seven minutes ringing) he would be the first to say kind, encouraging words and make us feel that we hadn't totally let him down.

Although he had aspirations for the Pilton ringers to be Championship League ringers, his strong belief in valuing everyone's contribution, however ham-fisted, helped it be a happy tower. Tom rang in the only recorded peals (three hours of continuous ringing) rung by a local band. His name can be seen on two of the peal boards on the ringing chamber wall, one dated 1952 and the other 1998.

Even towards the end of his life, when he found climbing up the stairs to ring the bells really difficult, he somehow got himself into the ringing chamber. He always came on our annual ringing outings and enthusiastically joined in all our social events; he never let the Pilton ringers down.

These days we still say, "Wonder what Tom's face is like?" after one of our less successful ringing touches.

For many years, the Church and Chapel Bazaar or Christmas Fair arranged for Father Christmas to arrive in style, with presents for all the children. Alan Sweet, known for his enthusiasm for vintage cars, would arrive in one of his cars. In this photo from 1998, and in 1999, he came in a 1937 Austin 16. Alan also had Austin Sevens, steam engines in varying states of repair filling his house and a Walls Ice Cream tricycle which occasionally graced the field at Pilton Show, weather permitting!

Alan Sweet as Santa Claus, with his vintage 1937 Austin 16 car, on arrival for the Two Churches Christmas Fete in 1998

Pilton can not only boast world-class rock musicians but also classical musicians. Anne Goode's son David took part in and won several international organ competitions, in 1997 and 1998. After some years in the USA and freelancing, he is now Organist and Head of Keyboard at Eton College, where he presides over a unique collection of historic instruments and teaches some of the UK's most talented young organists; he combines this with a concert career that takes him around the world, as well as playing at the Proms and other British venues.

Jean Eavis, Michael's second wife, known to many as the mother of the Festival as it grew in popularity, died from cancer, far too young, in the spring of 1999. Rob Kearle, who worked closely with them since the '80s recalls:

Jean was considered mother to the Festival. Very much her and Michael doing it all together. She was a very strong woman and wouldn't suffer fools gladly. If you crossed her, watch out. If you got on well with her, she was absolutely fantastic. She had a good sense of humour, if you were on the right side of it, it was brilliant.

Jean and Michael Eavis at the Festival in 1989

Liz Elkin writes:

Among Ray Loxton's list of accomplishments he is known for his grave digging and TV and media offerings. A combination of these can be found in a short film on You Tube made by Mandy Briggs in 2010, entitled *A Grave Matter*.

Ray explained that not everything always goes to plan when grave digging. Ron Garland died in 1999. "Even the undertaker couldn't understand it, he gave me the measurements and he checked them, but at Ron Garland's funeral the coffin would not fit. There were a few stones sticking out and the coffin would not go down. Ron Garland was a friend of mine and I had attended the funeral as a mourner not as gravedigger. Well I had to hop down into the grave, in my suit, and pull out the stones to make room for the coffin, it worked out all right eventually. Do you know, over the years whenever I played a prank on Ron he always got the better of me and he kept it going to the last."

The Garlands had four sons named Matthew, Mark, Luke and John.

Millennium 2000

A group photograph taken by Ian Sumner on 27th May proved quite a challenge, taken from high up in the bucket of a fork lift truck! See if you can spot yourself

2000 *was welcomed in many different ways in the village. The New Year itself was seen in with a village party and fireworks, both at the Village Hall and a rival bash down at Worthy Farm. The distant Tor was lit up with a spiral of lights and appeared indeed magical. On 1st January, the bells rang out in a national celebration of bellringing. On the 17th there was wassailing in the Millennium Orchard.*

In January 2000, Vivien Goode officially opened the Bush Nursery, as she describes here:

The idea of Bush Nursery started when Ringwell House closed. I had been working in nurseries locally and now, as there was a clear gap in the market, I thought maybe, just maybe I could run my own. Weeks of planning turned into months.... the wheels of bureaucracy turn so slowly.

Part of Bush Nursery was converted, equipment bought, staff recruited. The Nursery opened in January 2000 and has grown up and flourished. I must mention the huge input of my mother Anne, without whose help and encouragement the venture may never have got off the ground. Anne was a much-loved part of the Nursery, until she passed away in 2005.

The Bush Nursery is now always full, many families have sent two, three or four children here and it is lovely to have the house used in this way. I am passionate in my belief that young children should have the chance to be children in their earliest years. Parents say their children find Bush their second home: one little boy wakes his father at 5am with shouts of "go Vivi's!" I hope to continue to provide this for many years to come.

Open Day at the Bush Nursery. From left are Anne Goode, Karen Hillier, Vivien Goode, Anna Tolhurst, three-year-old Olivia King and the Rev John Woolmer of Shepton Mallet

Robin Cade writes:
We lived in Pilton for 25 years and have been on many committees, introduced the pancake races along Bread Street in the '80s and instigated the History Group and the initial booklets on the village. I devised and obtained the Millennium Orchard and chaired the Millennium festivities, so we left our mark! The event saw the return of the Abbot to the Barn and Michael dressed as a Cardinal, where his relationship with Liz started and Michael told me that this introduction "justified the cost of the festivities!"

The main entertainment to mark the new decade was planned for a Millennium Weekend in late May, in what is almost synonymous with Pilton weather: torrential rain and MUD! A Medieval Fayre with jousting horses, falconry took place despite the weather, plus an atmospheric circular tent for the evening, where the Lord Abbot's banquet was held. Again, truth proved stranger than fiction, as Michael Eavis met his third wife, Liz, who had lived here for years. He recalls:
The Millennium celebration – I really enjoyed it. There was a budget. I agreed to put on the evening show in the marquee and Arabella's people were doing all the fun bits, all the troubadours and jugglers, medieval comedians etc. We were sitting on the top table, John Edmunds, Mark Cann, and the so-called Lord Abbot of Glastonbury. We were supposed to be dressed up as monks. But when I went to the Fancy Dress place to pick up my monk's outfit, she said "I've got a Cardinal's suit for you, because all the monks have gone." "That's a bit over the top," I said. Great red beacon on my head, I did look absurd – it's a bit big-headed for me, being a Methodist, suddenly I'm a Cardinal, sitting with the monks! She said, "It really suits you, I've saved it for you."

So we were all lined up, drinking a bit of mead. The woman behind me had come in at the wrong place, so she climbed through the tent, having untied the strings to get in because she couldn't find the right entrance. So I picked her up and plonked her on the trestle table because she was on the wrong side and couldn't get through and she'd arranged to be with the Turners. I asked her for a kiss. This was Liz, dressed up as one of Henry VIII's wives, I think. What sealed it for me when we met again was her sense of humour.

They were married the following year, in August 2001 at the Methodist Chapel, in a non-Festival year, while all sides worked to ensure the future of the event and improve safety and security.

A Millennium Pageant was organised on the theme of 2000 years of village life, in song and verse devised by Ken Dilkes. The Millennium Pageant had to be held in the Club at short notice, due to muddy conditions on the Fayre site. Ken Dilkes wrote a work loosely based on history and research by Cecil Townsend. Pilton Players cast included Tom Capes, John Boucher, Ollie Jenkin, Patrick Sumner, Wendy Lynn, Madron Osborne, Ken and Jean Dilkes, Leena Shaw.

As part of the

PILTON 2000 **CELEBRATIONS**

PILTON PLAYERS

invite you to join them
for a light-hearted look at ......

2000 YEARS OF PILTON'S HISTORY
! ! !

COME TO THE ABBEY BARN MARQUEE

9PM SUNDAY MAY 28TH

Admission FREE !

PILTON 2000 PRESENTS THE

Pilton Mediaeval Fayre

At Cumhill, Pilton, Somerset

27th, 28th & 29th May, 2000
Noon until 5.30pm

Souvenir Programme

20p

Millennium Pageant poster   *Millennium Fayre poster*

As a Millennium project, Candace suggested there should be photos of all villagers outside their houses, either supplied by them or taken by her. Many were displayed at that year's Pilton Show. Space in this volume means we cannot possibly include them all, so please don't be offended if not in these examples.

Frank & Enid Challener

The Whatford family

The Austin family

Reg & Wendy Lynn

The Howe family

The Boucher family

The Sherwood family

The Mnatzagehnian family

The King family

Ruth Eavis and extended family

The Scotlands at Springfield

Margaret Drew and Rita Ayres devised a village tapestry. They write:

After several preliminary meetings to discuss a Millennium project, a few of us found ourselves with a tapestry to produce. Most of us could stitch, some would have a shot at design but none of us had ever tackled anything like this.

It was autumn 1995 (and we thought we had plenty of time) when we started to discuss and plan how to achieve a good result, yet still enable non-stitchers to contribute, as well as the more experienced needlewomen. It needed to be reasonably large, which would be difficult to work in one piece, so we arrived at a central map idea, surrounded by 18 small pictures of Pilton buildings. We wanted to get examples of old, new, grand and more modest dwellings. All this took many hours and gallons of coffee to finalise!

On 5th March 1996 we had a visitor from Mendip Arts and Leisure who advised us regarding costs. We also took names for help in drawing the designs. In March 1998 we purchased materials, after several forays into sourcing these and alternative designs, and framing costs.

Rita designed and produced the central map. She walked all the lanes and fields, noted where there were trees and walls; every single dwelling was marked and then she stitched it. Margaret undertook

Margaret Drew with the Millennium tapestry, now permanently in the church

the small picture kits, 18 of them. The photographs were taken and after selecting a balanced range were printed on a grid by George Milne, so we had our charts to work from.

Pilton Show Grants Committee awarded us £500: we were ready to go. Each square of canvas was fixed to an individual frame and appropriate coloured wools and a chart completed the work pack. Off went our teams of stitchers. Some did more than one picture, others did the basic stitching, leaving the detail to be completed by a more experienced stitcher. They all did very well: it was a good community project. We took the unfinished work to Pilton Show for people to put a stitch or two into the work: 77 people took up this offer.

The most difficult task was putting the whole thing together. Rita and Margaret spent a lot of time on either side of a large frame, stitching one stitch at a time to unite the map with the frame of 18 pictures. Once complete, it had to be framed: more research into pricing but we finally decided to make it really a Pilton product and asked David Drew to make the frame.

Completion was a little late, for 2000 had come and gone but finally the tapestry found a home in the Parish Church, where we hope it will give pleasure for years to come. It would not have materialised without the help of our team of stitchers: Rita Ayres, Gerry Barnes, Jane Boucher, Barbara Cade, Jean Dilkes, Margaret Drew, Sandra Howe, Wendy Lynn, Janet Raynsford, Jean Skidmore.

The downside of the new Millennium was that the Festival in 2000 saw an estimated 250,000 people attend, when only 100,000 tickets were sold. The large number of gatecrashers led to concerns for public health and safety and a serious rethink around licensing issues: Mendip refused any further licences until problems could be resolved. Enter Melvin Benn and his then company of events promoters, Mean Fiddler, who took over the public face of ensuring safety and security conditions were complied with. Under the umbrella of different companies, he continued in this role until 2012. His companies also run the Reading, Leeds, Latitude and Big Chill festivals. However, behind the scenes, according to Rob Kearle:

Michael had already designed the super-fortress fence before he'd signed up Melvin and Dick Vernon wrote the 2002 licence and had done the lion's share of that work. Mark Cann was very involved too. Melvin pulled it all together and was good at that; Michael has the people skills, doing deals over a handshake.

Testing the new security fence in 2000

Thus, from 2002 until 2012, the Festival was under much tighter control, with a higher, more secure fence and much better security. The idea of other larger, more commercial festival organisers being involved gave rise to all kinds of rumour-mongering. Again, numbers increased and Topsy grew larger and larger, spreading into new areas on site, with the fantasy worlds of Shangri La, Lost Vagueness and Trash City. Some of the strange recycled metal machines designed by Mutoid Waste Company's creator, Joe Rush, featured in the 2012 Paralympic Games closing ceremony. You saw it first in Pilton years before!

Joe Rush and one of his creations outside the Chapel, taking bride Emily Eavis to the reception down at Worthy after her wedding in 2009

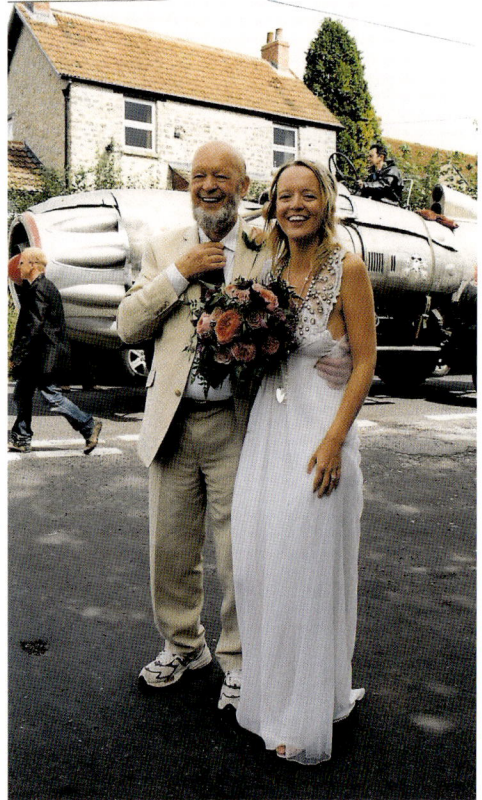

Michael Eavis and daughter Emily in front of the original going away vehicle

2001 saw the first of many awards to Brown Cow Organics, the company set up at the 480 acre Perridge Farm established by Judith's father, Douglas Turner. She and husband Clive Freane took over the dairy herd in the '90s. The concept grew from friends' responses to eating the beef born, bred and grazed on the farm, a cross breed of Guernsey dairy cow mother and beef bull father. They entered the 2001 Organic Food Awards and won against stiff competition. David Lidgate of the famous butchers, Lidgates on Holland Park Avenue, London considered it "some of the finest he had ever tasted." Over a decade later, they are still supplying Lidgate and have won numerous awards, selling direct through a website, at farmers' markets, events and from the farm by appointment only.

They never shoot bull calves, as some farms do, instead rearing the herd males though to adulthood. Judith said "animal welfare is a priority in everything we do and all the food we produce."

Judith & Clive Freane with Brown Cow Organic's prize-winning Guernsey herd

Brown Cow have now diversified into marketing their own artisan produced organic yoghurt, using their own whole milk. There is also River Cottage yoghurt, indirectly conceived when Hugh Fearnley-Whittingstall tried a sample of beef.

This success story has resulted in the farm producing 8,000 pots of yoghurt per week in 2012. Later in this decade, Judith began producing handbags, luggage and accessories from the cow hides, along with selling the complete hides as rugs or hangings.

Since 2001, they have won 31 awards for their organic beef and dairy products. Douglas must be smiling, thinking of the first few Guernsey cows he bought back in the 1950s.

In January 2002, one of the oldest papergirls in the country finally retired, aged 82. Great-grandmother Ella Blacker decided it was time to have a lie-in instead of delivering newspapers for the last 20 years, come rain, shine or even snow.

Ella Blacker

2002 was marked by the Queen's Golden Jubilee, celebrated with a church service, then on the Playing Fields in colourful style with bunting and flags. A horse and cart took people for rides through the village. Tea, a barbeque, disco and finally fireworks provided fun for all ages.

Horse and cart going past Mulberry cottage

Horse and cart leaving Pilton Church after the Jubilee service

The circus tent became a disco for the evening

Decorating the marquee, Gill Eavis, with Madron Osborne, Ruth Eavis, Jean Warry

Paul Warry and Ruth Eavis

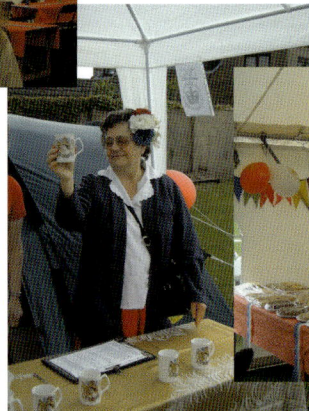

Rita Ayres and souvenir mugs

Margaret Drew and cakes

In October 2002, Lysbeth Ballantine was given the Save the Children Award for Distinguished and Meritorious Service by the charity's president, Princess Anne. She had devoted much of her time over 20 years to fundraising, following the shock of seeing children dying in Africa due to lack of supplies.

Richard Sheldon, former High Sheriff of Somerset, of Perridge House, also very involved with the Royal Bath and West Society, died in 2002. His daughter Emma (now Macdonald) together with friend Lucie Green, founded Bay Tree Foods in the kitchen at Perridge House in 1994. Both her parents helped with the company and his widow, Jennifer, continued to be involved while also raising large amounts for cancer charities. It is another of Pilton's success stories, winning gold awards in various tastings and going from strength to strength since early days when, in the '90s, certain Pilton houses gave out a strong aroma of herbs and spices, making sachets for mulled wine. Demand was such that they soon outgrew the kitchen table, expanded to Westcombe and an industrial unit near Thorner's at Pylle. Originally making relishes and chutneys, additionally today they produce dressings, preserves, marinades, sauces, oils, all made by traditional methods. Their wide range of products are now big business, in local and London food specialists and also sold online.

A stalwart of the village, George Windsor, also passed away in August 2002. First involved with the Legion Flower Show and Fete in 1947, some 50 or more years later, he was still involved, in its new guise. He was the crucial person who knew how to put the stalls together, stored at Burford, where he worked for the Bonds as a gardener. A new Legion standard was given in his memory in 2003. In recognition and thanks for all his work connected with Pilton Show, a bench was placed on the Playing Fields, inscribed with his name. In 2002, Philip Eavis passed the baton of running the Pilton Show to an unsuspecting Hugh Berry, who still holds this role some ten years later.

Kathleen Milne was always to be seen at the Flower Show and indeed, for many years, manned plant stalls at this and all other village fetes, fairs or Church spring or Christmas bazaars. A much-loved member of the community, she has a beautiful garden, at its best in spring with daffodils beside rushing water but colourful at any time of year. Generous in spirit and kind beyond measure, she has made curtains or furnishings for many houses in the village.

In April 2003, Michael Eavis sent a round robin letter to all village residents, reassuring everyone of Glastonbury Festival's intentions, concerning planning permission. The wording of the planning application gave cause for concern that other events might be staged at Worthy. Michael's letter ended: "if this festival is not run to the satisfaction of the local people then I will retire gracefully!" To date, both are still going strong.

Following a stroke after hedge laying in March 2000, Douglas Turner started to talk about his life to his family, after his eldest grand-daughter Heather did a school project with him talking about his life. Douglas was very keen to tell the whole story, so eventually, over the last two years of his life, Douglas would sit with his eldest daughter Shannon gathering the material for his lifestory 'Five Farms, A Somerset Farmer's Life,' which was published not long after he died as a promise to Douglas that it would go into print. Essentially "a simple record of a man who was fortunate enough to spend his life doing what he loved, and primarily a family history" it recounts how "his life revolved around farming; he had been involved in five farms throughout his life. With him through much of this was his much-loved wife Gwen, who pushed him through a period of expansion and allowed him to pass on a worthy legacy of farms and land to his children."

After his memorable funeral in 2003, the hearse led by a beautiful dark Shire horse, Shannon Turner describes how, once back at Perridge Farm:

A few of us were left and we started preparing a meal together. Clive had been up the top of the yard, doing a few chores around the farm, and suddenly he called out for us, and the siblings and children hurried up to where he stood. We looked towards where he was pointing and there, in a perfect arch, was a double rainbow – spanning the land.

The land, his land, has proved a fine legacy for Organic Vet Steve Turner and wife Kate, whose successful Party Packs business has now outgrown the sheds at Old Burford, and moved to industrial units at Westbury-sub-Mendip and also for the Guernsey herds producing the milk and beef for the Freane's Brown Cow Organics.

In September 2003, newcomer Maurice Davies spoke at the traditional Thanksgiving Service after Pilton Show, about his impressions of the village:
I should say straight away that Christine and I both feel that we have joined a warm and welcoming community. Having lived abroad, although we were aiming at Dorset or Wiltshire because we had lived there before, we are, as you can see, now in Somerset, a new county for us but one we are quickly learning to appreciate. Why this choice? These things are very hard to quantify but, as well as meeting most of our requirements, the house and its surroundings felt right.

We visited this Church on a Sunday afternoon. First and foremost it was open! Inside it is not only very beautiful but showed us signs of an active church and village life. As strangers looking to get a feel for the village, a couple of things stood out. Firstly the copies of the *Roundabout* magazine with all its information and, secondly, the red folder which, I hope, is still over there on the chest in the North aisle – full of more good information on who does what, where and when in the village – even including and appropriately for today, details of the Pilton Weekend. It was clear to us that somebody cared!

It is, as I have said, a warm and welcoming village with lots going on and typified by the activities of the last few days, but, as we all know, we are hosts to a world-famous event and this brings its own benefits and challenges. Inevitably it casts a shadow over many of the things we try to do as a community. Having said that, on a hot day, some shadow can actually be a benefit, so I am not being negative! Many other projects run and succeed alongside the festival. The superb alterations recently completed here in Church are one example, the Playing Fields, Gabriel's Orchard, the Tithe Barn and the Working Men's Club are others.

I allowed myself to be co-opted onto the Trustees for the Village Hall and knew the refurbishment project had a long and chequered history but I felt it was an area where a newcomer might be able to contribute. As well as raising funds in the village, we have to apply to a whole range of outside agencies for grants. My view is that, to do this successfully, the Trustees and the wider village community need to be in a position to present a united front to the outside world. To this end, my motto would be, internal debate, external solidarity. At least that's my impression as a newcomer!

In October 2004, old timer Teddy Stone's funeral proved a memorable occasion for John Fletcher:
Teddy Stone was the only son of farmers in the farmhouse on Lambert's Hill. Educated at the Cathedral School, he spent his life reading books as the farm crumbled around him. He could quote verbatim from the particular page of a particular book he'd been reading on a particular morning 23 years before.

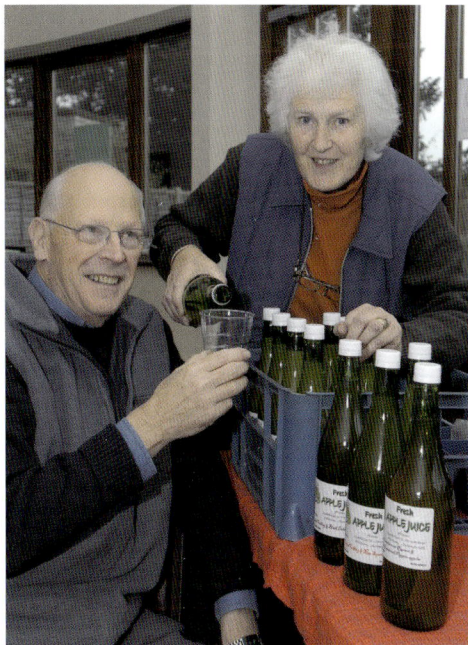
Maurice and Christine Davies at the Green Fair 2008

He was an extremely gentle and patient and generous individual. A Buddhist. He had artistic inclinations and used to put on avant garde theatre productions at Pilton Village Hall starring Margaret Miles and John le Carré. As he grew older he became more and more involved with the cats which surrounded him.

The cats multiplied greatly and slowly drove him out of the house, so he moved into his Mini car in the driveway. Gradually they drove him out of that, so, to give them more space, he moved from one new Mini to another followed by a relentless tide of ever more interbred cats, all the time vegetation growing into and around the derelict cars and trees growing in and out of the windows of the farmhouse. Travellers and friends started to live in caravans around the house.

So his funeral, when it came, was quite an event. (In Yeovil Hospital, as he was dying, he'd pulled all the catheters and medical paraphernalia out of his body, explaining he wished to die naturally).

A stolid phalanx of farming relatives occupied the front two or three pews in the church. For themselves the vicar provided a traditional hymn or two and the customary prayers.

Then there was the village further back in the pews. Patrick Eavis, in his broad Somerset preacher's twang, gave a spirited evocation of his and Teddy's youth, when Patrick had been veering towards severe Marxism but Teddy had cogently argued him into the gentler ways of anarchism.

And finally in the side aisles and jumping and dancing in and out of the main door and roving restlessly about were the travellers and mystics and Glastonbury individuals who simultaneously held their own impromptu memorial for Teddy, chanting, humming, rolling on the floor.

It was just the sort of service Teddy would have loved.

That same year, Jim Govier retired after 30 years as Chairman of Pilton WMC, only to become its president and probably just as active as ever.

During this time, tricky negotiations concerning funding were under way concerning the Village Hall and Club. Finn Christensen was Chairman of the

Andy Reilly with Jim Govier

Trustees and wrote to everyone explaining the position concerning fundraising. Meanwhile, the restoration scheme for the Tithe Barn was also running up against the buffers in terms of costs and time delays, the latter due to perfectionism in the craftsmanship of getting it all to the finest standards.

Ultimately solutions were found in the form of grants from the Heritage Lottery and contributions from Glastonbury Festivals and this decade saw the opening in successive years of these major projects.

The Tithe Barn was officially opened in 2005 on April Fool's Day, 1st April by renowned military historian, the late Sir John Keegan, wearing his Heritage Lottery hat for the occasion. He had tubercolosis as a child which affected one hip, so he always walked with a stick. In his latter years, he was confined to a wheelchair, as he was on Opening Day.

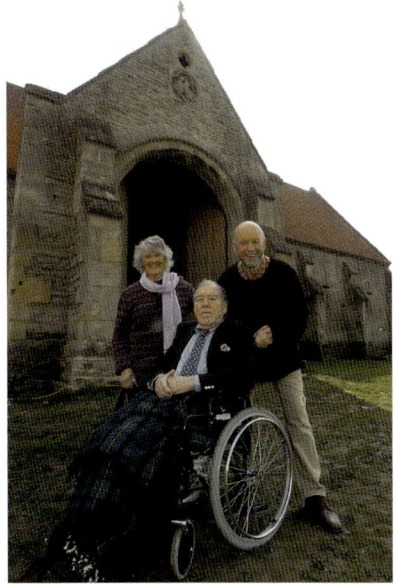

Official opening of the Tithe Barn on 1st April 2005 by the late Sir John Keegan, in wheelchair

According to Rob Kearle, one of the Barn Trustees:
When he first met Michael up there at the derelict Barn to decide whether the Lottery should fund it or not, he walked up to Michael and tapped him on the leg with his walking stick and said, "Yes, you'll get it to happen, won't you?" It was as if he was checking a piece of wood had woodworm or rot, as if to say, you're strong enough to see this through.

The restoration project gained national acclaim by winning in two categories, Structural and Best Use of British Timber, at the prestigious Wood Awards held at Carpenter's Hall in London. The judges considered it "a superb example of workmanship backed up by detailed research. To work on timbers the size of the ones used here, and to maintain the tolerances that they have, is a testament to the carpenters involved." Leader of the team working on it, Peter McCurdy, was responsible for the reconstruction of the Globe Theatre in London. Architect Jonathan Saunders of Caroe and Partners in Wells was project architect. Building started in 1999 and the roof is made of huge green oak timbers; there are more than 250 curved and shaped timbers, each differing in size and shape. Local archaeologists were all involved at the beginning, as was John McCutcheon, one of the early and continuing Trustees.

Michael was quoted at the time as saying:
I would have to say that this is one of the things I have done in my life that I am most proud of. The Barn belongs to the village and it is very satisfying to know the Festival has put something back into Pilton.

He confirmed this in 2012, rating achievements, saying:
The Tithe Barn stands out for me but my mother thinks the social housing is much more important than anything else.

Molly Gingell is a near neighbour to the Barn:
When Godfrey and I came to live in Pilton in 2000, we would often walk up to the top of Cumhill, where there was an ancient but roofless Tithe Barn and also a large Dutch barn. As the years have gone by, the latter has been replaced by Michael and Liz's amazing new house and the Tithe Barn has been re-roofed and restored. Watching this work in progress was a wonderful experience. As the great oak timbers were put in place, we were able to climb up a ladder and look at the incredible craftsmanship taking place, which was quite remarkable.

   In the fullness of time, this beautiful building was completed and the entire village was invited to the opening ceremonies. I especially recall masses of residents sampling generously provided drinks and wonderful cheeses, and a great party ensued where we all sat on bales of hay and thoroughly enjoyed ourselves.

The new Village Hall was officially opened on September 16th 2006, with David Heathcoat-Amory cutting the ribbon and smiles all around. Finn Christensen was quoted as saying, "The new Village Hall is a tremendous asset to Pilton." According to one press report, it was a "rousing speech" by Mary Renner that won the case to rebuild the hall centrally within the village, whereas alternative sites were hotly debated.

In February 2007, Mary, one of the founders of Happy Circle, passed away. This is extracted from Jean Dilkes appreciation of her:

Official opening of the new Village Hall by David Heathcoat-Amory in 2006

Mary was a loveable lady; a staunch royalist; great on punctuality, with strong ideals of life – although you did not always have to agree with her! Always good for supporting a cause. I can remember taking her to see our MP, David Heathcoat-Amory, when there was some concern about how many buses were going to be taken off. He listened!

Mary was a great supporter of the Friday Yeovil bus. Come hail, rain or shine, off she went, clutching the CLIC money collected at the Club. Over the years, Mary must have taken hundreds of pounds to CLIC. We must also keep up the tradition!

Another loss in 2007 was the premature death from cancer of Arabella Churchill, founder of Children's World charity, which grew out of the Festival. A new bridge in her memory was built on the Festival site over the Whitelake River, called Bella's Bridge, and opened in 2010.

In 2007, Michael Eavis went to Buckingham Palace, for once not wearing those famous denim shorts but dressed in a smart suit:
I got the C.B.E. which was quite a thing, I suppose. I've met the Queen a few times now and she was very well briefed on the Festival. She was so chatty about it and asked me loads of questions. She takes your hand and pushes you when you've got to go. The Master at Arms said when she does that, you have to move on. So I got the push, because I was talking too much, I suppose – questions require answers, don't they? You can't just say, yes or no, ma'am!

I was walking down as it was my turn and there was a Beefeater all dressed up in fancy gear, who said "Neil Young next year, please!"

Indeed, Neil Young played Pilton in 2009. When asked if there's a band that he'd like to have play the Pyramid Stage, who have never played, Michael answered "Well, I would like the Stones: we've had everyone else! But I haven't got much hope for that to happen...."

2007 was one of the wettest, muddiest, flooded out Festivals and thousands of tents were left behind in the aftermath. The clear-up took months, cost £800,000 and also left serious question marks over the whole event. Fortunately the following year '08 was a dry one, and Rob Kearle, who had an army working on the clear-up, said "When the weather is good, everything is easier. We have had only about 10% of the tent problem. People took away much more and we have about half of the ordinary rubbish of last year. And our new recycling centre in the barn is working a treat." Two specialist recycling firms are now involved in the massive operation, as festival attendance figures on paper were 177,500.

Police search and rescue divers were brought in to check flooded tents in 2005

Robert Kearle describes the whole process of clearing up after what looks like a deserted battlefield and how it's evolved over the years:

The odd thing about the clear-up is that we knew the recession was coming a year before it actually hit. We knew we were in a boom before, because we couldn't get people to come and do litter picking. But we were inundated with mainly young people, in late teens early 20s, who just couldn't get work. They were coming from everywhere, all over the country as well as from Europe, they were saying, there's no work, we haven't had any work for six months. This was when the country was still booming. So you knew a recession was coming. Oddly enough, a recession's very good for us because people want work, whereas a boom's really bad for us. People have too much money, they can holiday abroad.

We don't sign people up long-term, it's on a daily basis. If they turn up, they get work. If they don't, they don't. There's a large turnover of people, there's a huge camp. The work is so hard, so dirty, so messy, you get lots of people who just can't hack it, who think they're going to have a jolly and a bit of a party but in fact it's not like that. It's like a military operation, they're lined up in a field. There's bags, there's gloves, there's supervisors behind you, there's people behind you giving out more bags. You fill bags full of rubbish. You have a break mid-morning, you have a lunch break and you work the afternoons, then you have your dinner. It's working in a regimented way, field by field, that's how you break it up. If you look at the whole site, 1,400 acres or so, how the hell do you do it? You work it out. We always start in the Pyramid field and the ones by the village. Then there's a whole host of other teams, people on tractors and trailers picking up the wood, metal, stone, dustbin carts picking up the bags.

We have about 1,500 during the show, mainly volunteers. Afterwards on any one day as many as 600 working, probably going through about 1,000 overall. Some people will only do a day or two to get the train fare home, others have a purpose to earn more. The strange thing about it is the best litter pickers tend to be girls in their late teens to mid-20s. They're doing it for a purpose, whereas the boys are just here for a party and it's quite difficult to get them to work. The girls are very focused, with an objective, whether it's for college or Uni, or to get the car repaired. There's a real gender difference.

It evolves every year. Last year I had an email and a phone call from a police officer, accusing us of stealing abandoned tents because they still belonged to people who left them there. I went, "OK this is going to be interesting. Strange idea, you leave something behind and it's theft." To start off with, there's anywhere between 500 and 2,000 people on the Sunday night and Monday after the Festival going round campsites picking up abandoned tents, abandoned chairs. They will be crew, locals, land owners – so you're going to have a hard job finding out who took what tent. It was *nonsense*! You get a policeman with a bee in the bonnet and you often get nonsense come out.

Obviously we get lots of charitable groups, from Scouts, boys' clubs, to village halls. We've had a village hall get tents because they were going to use them as bags to fill with sheeps' wool for insulation on their new roof! May sound odd but 50 years ago that's what everyone did.

We probably have to up to 50 of those groups. Some will only take half a dozen, some will take 50 or 60 tents. Some will want frying pans, sleeping bags, Lilos, clothes. That's always been the case. I remember 20 years ago now, one of the first years I did litter picking, it was much smaller then, there was this one girl and she was just collecting pairs of jeans. It was a muddy Festival and people had left their muddy jeans behind. She had a big van and she was taking them off site and I thought, saves us, we were only going to throw them away.

One day, I was chatting to her. She said she had an occasional stall at Camden Market in London. "I take these jeans, it costs me £1 a pair to have them washed, dried and ironed." That was in the days when jeans were expensive. She said she sold them for £20 a pair in Camden Market. She'd made in excess of £20,000 , from just left over jeans!

Rob Kearle and litterpickers with some of their finds

Robert House summed up the detritus of earlier Festivals and the waste left behind: "If you're a Nomad, you can't carry anything..." When clearing up electrical equipment, they'd found endless jars of Branston Pickle and huge chunks of Cheddar cheese amongst other things!

In 2007, the village lost its Post Office on the main road, transferring business to what initially appeared to be a small cupboard in the Village Hall, run with staff from Glastonbury Post Office.

In March 2008, Dave Chapman made his exit from life's stage. His niece Suzanne Millard, Ann's daughter, wrote an appreciation, read by Ken Dilkes, from which this is taken:

Please don't remember him as the frail, old-before-his-time man he had become at the end. Remember him as the man with the big, booming laugh. Remember him as the man who loved and lived in Pilton all his life. Remember the handsome young man who proudly carried the Pilton British Legion's standard for many years, and latterly served with distinction on the Branch's committee. Remember the young man who was, for a while, the village milkman, and let the kids ride on his milk float.

Remember the man who drove over his lunch box in his fork lift truck, on more than one occasion. Remember the man who picked up all the nieces and nephews, late at night, after parties. Remember the man who quietly and unobtrusively tended the gardens of those no longer up to the task, and helped them in other practical ways. Remember the man you couldn't get away from when he stopped you for a chat (he could talk for England). Remember the man who sang and danced his way through many Pilton Players productions, though he was no Frank Sinatra. Remember the man who put the 'happy' into the Happy Circle. Remember the man who loved his Methodist Christian faith and sang loudest at Chapel. Remember him as the great, much loved villager that he was.

Doors close, doors open. A new resident arrived that March, Guy Kennaway, a successful novelist, as well as writing columns for national newspapers. Being well-versed in fiction, in an earlier draft, he imagined the former owner as a Colonel, which made entertaining reading but was factually incorrect. Perhaps he had heard of aforementioned retired military, or of Scotch Corner, as that part of John Beales Hill was known, with Frasers, Fraser-Mackenzies and McNeills descended from Scottish clans:

I arrived in Pilton in 2008 on a watery March evening. When you move into a house you often get an idea of the people who lived there before you, from the way they set the place up, from what they took with them and what they left behind. You see all their modernisations, improvements, and additions. The last family who lived in Grey Gables had I think four boys, and as I cleared the garden and clumsily arranged a new one I keenly felt their summer games and playful hours in the undergrowth where amongst the rotting leaves I found in total 36 balls of one shape or another. These balls varied in age from new and hard to mouldy and soft, and each represented the end of a particular game,

which had culminated in a fruitless search for the ball, and preceded the trooping into the house for tea, or whatever, now they had nothing to play with. These were the Morris-Adams children and parents, but the owners before them had left behind a more indelible mark on the house.

The Morris-Adams family at Grey Gables

This was a man I know just as Mr Fraser, and his wife The Honourable Mrs Fraser. I never met either, but apparently he was a diligent land agent. No one I spoke to ever said her name without The Honourable prefix. She had insisted on it. She bought the rectangle of land on the edge of my garden from her neighbour in Pilton House for a tennis court. On my walks around the village, I noticed at least three other grass courts of the same period, which conjured up in my imagination a lively society of mixed doubles in Edwardian costume, with old wooden rackets and jugs of Barley Water. While The Honourable Mrs insisted on strict title protocol, Mr Fraser pursued his own hobby: laying concrete. Grey Gables, a gentle medieval building, was covered in the stuff. The Fraser swimming pool was like a nuclear bunker without the roof. When I came to removing it, the JCB driver said, "How thick is that concrete on the bottom? Can't be more than five inches, six at the most, you wouldn't need more than that." It took him two weeks to get through three feet of reinforced concrete. You could have built The Shard on it. It was as though Mr Fraser lived in constant fear of a 200 pound bomb being dropped on the place.

There was an alarming level of security in the house, continuing the slightly paranoid theme of the concrete. Mr Fraser had fitted two wall safes, one big enough to run a small bank from, and heavily barred all windows. All of which made me wonder what exactly it was that Mr Fraser was so scared of. Who was he keeping out? Unless of course the bars were to imprison his wife, who, maddened by the desire to play tennis and enforce correct nomenclature, would escape the house at any time if she wasn't fully secured, with her ankle length pleated tennis skirt, tennis racket and copy of Debretts.

It wasn't long before I was told: the security was in place because of the hippies who came to the Festival. I remember sitting in my pretty well empty house when I first got to Pilton and answering the door to a nice lady – I have no idea who she was – carrying a clipboard. I invited her in and wanting to be friendly said I'd sign her petition. There were eight names on it, and the rubric across the top read something like: "We the undersigned abhor the Glastonbury Festival and call for its immediate cessation." I think I signed; she wasn't a woman to be trifled with. Anyway, if the bars were anything to go by, it was a jolly good thing to stop.

In the event, I discovered that the weeks around the Festival turned the village into something like a Californian gated community: I think I even had my own security guard for a few days, who saluted me semi-ironically every time I drove in and out. The village was ringed with young men and women in security tabards, who on the last day of the Festival deserted their posts leaving smouldering fires and empty chairs, like the retreat from Moscow. Reinforced window bars seemed somewhat excessive, so they had to go.

As for the Festival site: hardly a hippy in view, just lots of people like me, well off, middle aged, long past being groovy. After a couple of Festivals, I discovered that the Glastonbury Festival is a summer activity like tennis and cricket, for which rain should stop play. It is charming to attend when the ground is hard and you can lie on the grass and talk and play, but in that oily mud under sheeting rain it was torture, and I never understood how or why the punters pretended it was different, and with such enthusiasm. When it rained during the 2011 Festival I pretended to my house guests that I had lost my ticket and couldn't get onto the site. I watched them search my house from top to bottom while it burnt in my back pocket. I shoved them out of the door, told them to enjoy themselves and went to sit on my own with a whisky in front of the fire listening to Radio 4, feeling very grumpy about the world. I felt at that moment that the Frasers would have at last approved of me.

As a sometime guest of Malcolm and Elizabeth Fraser, who were very kind to my father after my mother's untimely death, I know nothing of hidden layers of concrete. The Hon. Mrs is technically correct, being the daughter of a Peer of the Realm, the fifth Lord Methuen. Her brother inherited the title but he died in 1994. The Frasers moved to Corsham to be near the family seat, Corsham Court, now used by Bath Spa University for post-graduate studies and for study of the arts, humanities and culture.

The house Guy moved into was far older than 20th century concrete. Tod Morris-Adams recalls how:
Michael Chapman, a friend and conserver of old buildings, was repointing a section of the stonework. He reached into a pudlock (hole in the building used as a primitive scaffolding point) and pulled out a diary left by the owner in 1696. It is still legible and now able to be seen in Wells Museum, opposite the Cathedral.

A newcomer became active in the village: Kelly Sumner became chairman of the Working Men's Club and with Andy Reilly organised regular young bands slots for live music at weekends. Kelly describes meeting one of Pilton's best-known characters:
When we moved in, there were stonemasons working here for about eight months. One day, they were working on the bridge over the stream and I was taking them out cups of tea, stopping to chat. They said, "Brother Ray says there are otters in this stream." I wondered who this "Brother Ray" was, perhaps one of their brothers or a wandering monk?

A while later, someone came to the door saying could they look around and see if there was any wood. I took him around the fields and we were chatting for about 20 minutes. I realised he had said "brother" about 200 times and that this must be "Brother Ray."

In May 2008, the Tithe Barn saw a very different and original use for the interior, remote yet linked to its agricultural beginnings. An art exhibition by Bill Leyshon, self-taught portrait painter, brother of Liz who runs the all-important Strode Theatre, and Nell, a playwright, filled it with larger than life sized paintings of local Somerset characters, in a series of 'Men Who Work,' connecting people to the pulse of nature and landscape. In the catalogue, he wrote:

The Tithe Barn seems the perfect place to give weight to these paintings, which are hung to appear as if stained glass windows in a church.

He also painted smaller portraits to commission and for a couple of weeks, welcomed all who visited. It was the start of more varied uses for the Barn.

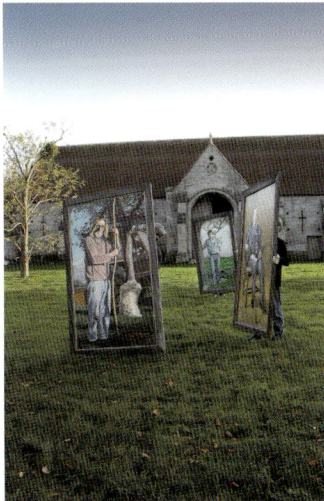

Interior of the Tithe Barn during the portraits exhibition

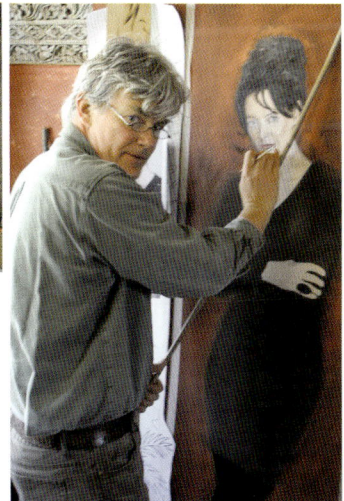

Life size paintings ready for Bill Leyshon's exhibition in the Tithe Barn 2008

Bill Leyshon at work on a portrait

During the 2000s, Candace moved from Ebenezer to The Dell, where according to Radio Bristol, she continues "working in a green oasis." Her studio and garden are certainly one of the main attractions during Somerset Art Weeks, a riot of colour and imagination. In 2008, the Victoria Art Gallery in Bath held an exhibition of her mosaic work on the theme of 'Blue and White' together with textile artist Carole Waller's fabrics. Yet a little known fact is that she also helped as a volunteer at Shepton Mallet Prison, as she describes:

As an outsider, I can jump in where others fear to tread. Security problems don't bother me, I'm not fearful of the men. I was committed to the whole thing: they developed their creative skills, their growing and interaction skills and became very proud of their work. Some of them won prizes at the Koestler Awards in London for their needlepoint. We had an exhibition at Strode. They created their own designs. Those eyes *(pointing at an intricately detailed work)* were by the most creative boy, he just sat down and did them. When I praised him and praised him, he just looked down and one of the prisoners said, "He doesn't know what to do with that praise, Candace. We've never been praised like that." I was there for four years.

Pilton Show weekend in 2008 tried combining the Rock Star '08 Battle of the Bands with the event, rather than holding a Pilton Party. This was organised by Kelly Sumner with Andy Reilly in somewhat of a baptism of fire. It was one of the wettest weekends of the year and the Flower Show and Barn Dance the following day were hit by monsoon weather, instilling a stiff upper lip and 'Show must go on' attitude. The Barn Dance became a 'welly dance,' water dripped

Annie Maw and prizewinners at Pilton Show 2008

everywhere and everyone adapted accordingly, with those best of weapons, goodwill and laughter. Philip Eavis was to be seen frantically attempting to sweep water out of the flooded marquee. Not a good year! As Philip subsequently said, "It should have been stopped, shouldn't it, as it's a miracle no one hurt themselves, but do we ever? The show must go on!" Everyone tried to save the situation and no one broke their leg.

The irony was that Annie Maw, then High Sheriff of Somerset, officially gave the prizes for the afternoon's Flower Show. It was the one year we had someone in a wheelchair (as a result of a hunting accident): she had to be lifted over the mud. As Philip recalls, "It was very hard on her. It was a memorable event in all respects, though perhaps not for the right reasons."

Hugh Berry, Chairman of the Show, recalls:
The 2008 show weekend remains large in my memory. It was the last time the marquee was at the bottom of the Playing Field, where it had been since the old Pavilion burnt down, so that we could hook up to Philip & Gill's nearby water and electricity.

After the Friday night event, all the equipment was loaded onto the van parked at the end of the marquee where it stayed overnight. Due to the amount of rain during the previous week and overnight, the ground was very soft and when the van tried to reverse out, it sank down in mud up to its axles. We had to get Kelly Smith in with his large machine to pull the vehicle out, leaving two trenches up the field. A couple of weeks later, I was summoned to a meeting of the Playing Field committee to explain how we were going to repair the ground.

Apart from that, I remember the day of the Show well. The morning was dry and we were hopeful it would remain that way for the rest of the day. The Show opened at 2pm as usual and at 2.20pm, the heavens opened. I was standing in the front of the marquee watching the surface water run down the field and, unlike King Canute, knowing there was nothing I could do to stop it. The jazz band,

Rain deluged the Playing Fields on the afternoon of Pilton Show 2008

The Wizards of Avalon, continued playing on the covered terrace of the Pavilion until it became too much for them as well. Everything possible had been moved inside the marquee which was pretty crowded, but we carried on. The Emporium had pitched camp inside the Pavilion but mud was everywhere. All the outside activities were cancelled, as were the activities planned for Sunday afternoon.

After a lot of hard work, laying of straw and coconut matting, the Village Supper and Barn Dance went ahead as planned although the footwear was not as normal. It has gone down in history as the 'Welly Barn Dance' remembered fondly by all who were there. By the end of the evening, there were some very muddy teenagers and we subsequently received a large bill from Adams Marquees for cleaning the tent, tables and chairs – not surprising really.

Needless to say, there have been many very enjoyable shows before and after but strangely enough, I have fond memories of that weekend.

Concerning the Show, Philip also says: The Show is about so many people, it's not about one person at all. When they talk about this great community spirit, it takes a lot of work to achieve it behind the scenes and a lot of commitment.

Rob Kearle is an unsung hero of so many things in the village: quietly gets on and does so much. *Other backstage heroes are Terry Moulder and Audrey Brown, so essential for this and other village events, running the bar all weekend and/or providing food, thus keeping everyone in good spirits, in all senses of the word. Not forgetting the tea ladies, formerly run by the WI but more recently organised by Gail Milne.*

Subsequently, Glastonbury Festivals staged an Equinox Party which a year later reverted to the Friday night slot, renamed (again) as the Pilton Party. Few villages can boast the line-up that has played for this event, bands in the early stages of their rise to stardom such as Coldplay and the Kaiser Chiefs have played on Pilton Playing Fields, prior to Olympics ceremonies and other international mega-spectaculars! Now the event has outgrown the marquee and is held on Worthy land. However, the rest of the weekend remains a traditional village show.

A younger Chris Martin played solo for Pilton Party in 2000 on the Playing Fields, without the rest of Coldplay, the year of their debut album 'Parachutes,' before they went global. Since then they have won numerous prizes, sold 55 million albums worldwide and in 2012 played for the Paralympics closing ceremony.

Rob Kearle remembers when the Stone Roses played on the Playing Fields, at that time one of the largest bands in the world, unable at the last minute to play the Festival. Everyone tried to keep it secret but "a virtual Who's Who of the music business came through the gate." Rob remembers a classic time when: For some reason we gave Michael the bag with all the cash in it from the gate money. He went off to get fish and chips for us on the gate, from the van on the field. When he came back, we said, "Where's the money?" He raced back and it was still on the ground by the van. Just as well, or that would have been £20,000 lost! From then on we didn't let him handle any money.

In September 2008, during Pilton Show weekend, a reunion was organised to mark the 50th anniversary of the closure of Pilton School. Hedley Lomas, whose stepfather was Alfie Connock, was there from 1948-54. About 60 former pupils had an enjoyable afternoon exchanging memories on a walk through the village, taking in the old school house, before a cream tea, provided, as for so many village occasions, by Gill Eavis and helpers.

Among former pupils gathered at the 2008 reunion: Pat Hill, Molly Dredge, Angela Henderson, Philip Eavis, Valerie Whatford, Diana Boyce, Ruth Eavis, Pat Darch, Michael Ball, Joy Salisbury, Neville Henderson, Hedley Lomas, James Dredge, Susan Eavis, Elizabeth Hill, Jim Govier, Ann Chapman

In 2008, Kate Lewis and her husband Andy set up the Pilton Pig at Tanyard Farm, starting with two Gloucester Old Spots sows and expanded their herd to around 35 pigs of varying ages, all traditional rare breeds. They concentrated on the rarest British breed, the Lop, a West Country pig, in an aim to help preserve this for future generations. Kate

Happy Pilton pigs

said they were passionate about preserving the traditional rare breeds and "As a family we love animals and have always been concerned about animal welfare with respect to meat production." They became well known for "fantastic bacon" and tasty sausages, as well as the pork itself and sold at farmers' markets and locally and direct from a small farm shop.

Kate said "Unfortunately due to the ever increasing price of pig food we have had to cease trading for the foreseeable future" so they ceased trading commercially in December 2011.

Pilton United celebrate their promotion

Pilton United football team had a good season for 2008/9 – they were promoted to Division Two of the Mid Somerset League. For 2009/10 they went one better and became champions of Division One, where they remain. Team captain Neil Davies is in the centre row, second from left.

The Allotments Group was formed in 2008: this photo taken in July 2009 was their first summer

In 2009 Keith Harlow, who had only recently completed his history of the village 'Aspects of Pilton,' suddenly died on the day it returned from the printers. A keen member of Pilton History Group, Keith spent many hours on the project, which looks at life in the village from the Bronze Age to the early 20th century.

For Somerset Art Week in 2009, a dramatic opening launch for an exhibition organised by Fay Rickwood made full use of the space of the Tithe Barn, with acrobats doing trapeze acts high above the assembled crowd. Devolution, aerial performance artists Gemma Michael and Darryl Carrington, had opened the Colston Hall the night before but this was the oldest place they had ever performed. Local artists on show included sculptor Sukey Erland, textile artist Jasmine Eavis, hides and accessories from Brown Cow and jewellery by Fay Rickwood, as well as other Somerset talent.

In December, Capt Oliver Truman, son of Jane and Paul, who Ruth remembers teaching at West Pennard School, spoke about his recent experiences in Afghanistan to a packed village hall, raising funds for the British Legion.

Listening to his first-hand experiences and seeing photos starker and more dangerous than those shown on TV news and in newspapers, of village house to house foot patrols and the sheer distances covered, brought home to everyone the impossibilities of that particular theatre of war. No one has ever beaten the Afghans, as history has proven. It was sobering that this message reached even this small Somerset village so powerfully and directly.

2010 onwards ...

The 'Big Lunch' on Sunday 3rd June 2012 in the Tithe Barn to celebrate the Queen's Diamond Jubilee

2010 saw turmoil in politics, leading to the current Coalition, and a change of local MP.

From many years of being a safe Conservative seat, Wells and surrounding area voted in a Liberal, Tessa Munt. The Tories succeeded in slinging almost as much mud in her direction for alleged past indiscretions (all unproven as it turned out) but this did not have as disastrous an effect as did the sacks of manure Roger Noble acquired for the garden at Beales House, which unfortunately entered into the whole bizarre parliamentary expenses scandal.

The Daily Telegraph, no less, shot many Tory MPs in the foot, causing mayhem for months on end and no doubt increasing its circulation. It was an understandably painful time for the MP's wife, Linda Heathcoat-Amory, a talented artist in her own right, who was very sad about it all. "Gardens are strange things, and that particular one was just getting good when I had to give it up, I really loved it and the area."

The beautiful garden that caused so much trouble

Painting by Linda Heathcoat-Amory of flowers in the garden

Philip Eavis was agent for the Liberals, as he had been for the last 20 years. He said:

The village is 50/50 as we know from canvassing – 50% Tory and 50% anti-Tory. That's not 50% Liberal. Most of the Labour people vote Liberal in this constituency. So the village has been quite political. All politics ends in tears.

Ruth's father's diaries of 1922 when the last Liberal was elected are interesting, he's got all this written down. My father and he were just as active as I am now in the campaign. They were twin brothers and my father, my grandfather were all very strong Liberals. It's a tribal thing. Yet Michael, Pat and Susan all left the tribe for Labour.

The Festival marked its 40th anniversary in many ways, not least with Stevie Wonder singing one of his hit songs, 'Happy Birthday' on stage with Michael and over 100,000 people! An exhibition at the Atkinson Gallery at Millfield for a month that summer showed a selection of photos over the years. This selection from photographer Ann Cook (overleaf) is mainly from the last 20 years but shows some of the energy and humour that has developed.

Before the Festival began, workers on site gave Michael a surprise 'drive by' parade, in a 60 vehicle carnival. Each van, car or other vehicle reflected an aspect of the site or part of the history.

It was also the year in which a beautifully-crafted bridge, for which the oak came from an old lock gate on the Kennet and Avon Canal, was officially opened across the Whitelake River on the Worthy Farm site, celebrating the life of Arabella Churchill. It is now known as Bella's Bridge, in recognition of her work providing creative, educational and social benefits for all children, through her charities Children's World, and its international arm, which grew out of the Children's Field. From 1981 she had been responsible for running the circus and theatre fields.

Asked why it all seems so much more streamlined and less trouble for the village, Rob Kearle, now on the Parish Council, said:
The initial meetings between Mean Fiddler and Parish Council went quite well, actually. A lot of good things were sorted out then, with the realisation that that kind of thing couldn't go on any more. Tripartite working between the Festival, Mendip Council and Avon & Somerset Police, as much as that's annoying for some people, really worked better. You can't beat your head against the Council and the Police. Fortunately it coincided with the economic boom, so money wasn't so much of an issue any more. So you could pay for more police, more security.

Sandra Howe, Chair of the Parish Council since 2007, said it was now far easier with more "co-operation not antagonism and a lot of compromise." Robin Clark, Chair from 2003-2007 after Ron Ballantine, paved the way for clearer co-operation and liaison.

Sheelagh Allen has manned the office at Worthy Farm since 1985 from the Festival's early days, through thick and thin, as Michael's essential right hand. She would have some amazing stories to tell, had she ever time enough to do so, with such a busy and demanding work schedule. Firmly rooted in the village, Sheelagh said, "What's important to me is that I was baptised, confirmed and married all in Pilton Church."

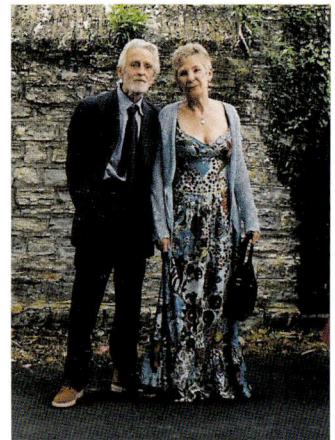

Sheelagh and John Allen at Emily Eavis' wedding in 2009

History of a different kind came to Pilton, as on 24th June 2010, a royal visitor arrived: Prince Charles came to officially open the low cost housing project at Oathills and John Burns Cottages. Afterwards, he made a surprise visit to the Festival, the day before music began, in his role as president of Water Aid, during which time he appeared briefly on the Pyramid Stage and toured the Greenpeace fields, looking far too tidy to be a proper festival goer. This would have been unthinkable 20 years earlier.

Michael describes how:

He was very keen to come to the Festival, because of William, I think. He was very impressed by all the craftsmanship at the Tithe Barn. I was showing

Prince Charles at Oathills 2010

him the wooden gates to the Barn, saying I'd got two of them. His reaction, oh, what's the public school word for bragging, "You *swanker...*" It was as if one farmer were speaking to another. He agreed they were good gates, though.

He made a nice speech and it did sound sincere: I was quite impressed with his sincerity. For once in my life, I didn't really know what to say.

It's a luxury to be able to choose craftsmen when you like what they do, even if it's not financially viable. So now I can attract all these people who make lovely hurdles and gates. We're employing the same carpenters at the moment because they've got incredible skills. I do appreciate people that can make things that I can't do myself, so I've got an obsession about giving them work. People who can do exceptional stuff are few and far between. There are stonemasons and wood carvers who are so clever, their skills so unique. Exceptional carving skills and woodworking like those gates, the ones Prince Charles thought I was bragging a bit too much about.

Prince Charles at the Festival 2010

I do spend a lot of money employing those people now. That's why the Green Craft Field is important to me, because those sort of skills are still very valuable to us.

Newcomers to the village, also interested in craft, making musical instruments, making and restoring furniture, Scott Baldwin and Clare Steadman arrived in 2010. In a previous life, they ran their own business, but now both feel they have joined 'a bigger team' and describe their first impressions:

Relocation has its perils, researching before you buy should avoid unpleasant surprises but one thing that you can never be sure about until you take up residence are the people, are the natives friendly?

Coming from an urban environment, used to an ever-present air of intimidation, we, like many others, followed a strategy of keeping ourselves to ourselves. In our last year in Rugby, there had been three serious armed robberies, numerous late night muggings, countless acts of vandalism and even a murder by stabbing, all within 200 yards of our house. The police helicopters with their searchlights were regularly hovering, we didn't ever walk the dog at night.

When moving time came, we researched all of our target areas thoroughly, reading local papers online, determined to get it right. Details of two houses in Pilton joined the growing pile, one of them had a very nice workshop. During one late night laptop hunt for more information I discovered the 'ASBO Team' on the *www.pilton.com* website. It was heart-warming and struck a chord with me; a group of locals freely giving their time to keep the village clean and tidy, like a group of ageing super-heroes with a refreshingly simple objective. We studied the website and decided the village seemed right for us. Miraculously, six months after first finding it, the house with the workshop was still for sale (thank you Credit Crunch!) We came to see it, we had lunch in the Crown, we came back in the pitch dark to check for 'hoodies'(incidentally, it never gets *this* dark in Rugby) and we made a purchase.

On arrival our immediate neighbour, who was just going out said, "I have left my house open, please go in and make a cup of tea, you will find everything in the kitchen, I will be back later." Passers-by stopped and exchanged pleasantries with us. A 'Welcome Pack' arrived; a copy of *Roundabout*, the Parish Rooms Centenary booklet, a footpaths map and some details about the Church. At the 'What's on in Pilton' day we were staggered by the range of interests followed and shared within the community. Everyone was so friendly, their enthusiasm was infectious, the hospitality and welcome shown to us as newcomers to the village was fantastic, we joined in.

Moving away from our large family network was a concern for us, would we feel isolated? Fortunately not, the village community is extensive, people are helpful, positive, social, they are interested, they care. If any hole was created when we moved, kind and friendly villagers have leapt in to fill it. And of course there are the 'characters,' the 'deeply held opinions' and the 'Festival,' which is a subject all of its own. Don't get me wrong, this is no Utopia, there is healthy debate and polarised opinion on a vast number of issues but having settled recently as an outsider I am struck by the inter-connectedness of all people here, indigenous locals and incomers of various longstanding. We have all joined a tribe.

My advice to anyone moving into a small community like ours is to make the effort and get involved. Joining in and helping each other develops and strengthens our social bonds. It enriches everyone's life and most importantly, our own.

Upheaval was also of a more earthy nature, according to Rob Kearle, Chairman of the Playing Fields Committee:
We levelled the Playing Fields in 2010 which had a 12 ½ feet fall from corner flag to corner flag originally, from by the gateway to down by the tennis court. Philip filmed the whole thing. We found thousands of fossils, ammonites, loads of people came to get them; we pulled up loads of marquee pegs that had got stuck in the mud. It proves it was under the sea many hundreds, millions of years ago.

We brought in another 2,000 tonnes of topsoil and must have moved 25,000 tonnes of rock in levelling it and put a lot of drains in it, too.

The unique Eric Hewer

In December 2010, the same night as the Carol Service in the Chapel, the village experienced an unexpected tragedy – ambulance sirens wailing in a snowy night meant that Eric Hewer, taken to hospital in emergency after a heart attack, was suddenly no more. John Fletcher's letter to Pat Hewer was read out at his funeral:
Dear Pat and Girls,
Paula ordered me to type this out because my handwriting is illegible, so apologies for the unnatural formality of this typed letter.

It is also unnatural to write about the death of someone like Eric who was so unnaturally full of unending and deeply improbable Life.

I know that, unlike me, you don't believe in life after death – and I'm already bracing myself for when I run into Eric in the afterlife – but Eric continues to live in so many ways in *this* life. Firstly, of course, through you and all of the girls. In fact, as the grandchildren arrive, you will all doubtless be playing "Spot the Eric."

But we mustn't forget the thousands of quite innocent, unwitting people Eric collided with in everyday life. A girl serving him his tobacco in a motorway 'Fags 'n Mags' whose view of life was irretrievably turned upside down by a single one-liner from Eric as he handed her the wrong money. The poor bloke stood next to him in a pub urinal whose brains were irrecoverably melted into new and alien life forms by a death-defying double-somersault in Eric's logic. Eric brought Life to many, many people, just by simply failing to shut up. Everyone will miss him terribly – but his generosity and wit march inexorably and ominously on.

That same thick spell of snow brought a happier memory. Artist Jasmine Eavis (née Moore) had returned to the village where she had spent some of her childhood, first of all aged two when her family rented accommodation at Worthy Farm, then at West Compton, then at nearby Parbrook. She married her childhood sweetheart, Paul Eavis, son of Philip and Gill but things didn't work out. She met another Paul while living in Street, while she was teaching art at Strode College, but wanted to move back to Pilton. Due to be married at Pylle church, the church for the Somerset Guild of Craftsmen, in whose churchyard her father is buried, the thick snow posed problems how to get the bride to the church in such treacherous, icy weather. Father Christmas came to the rescue, as Jasmine recalls:

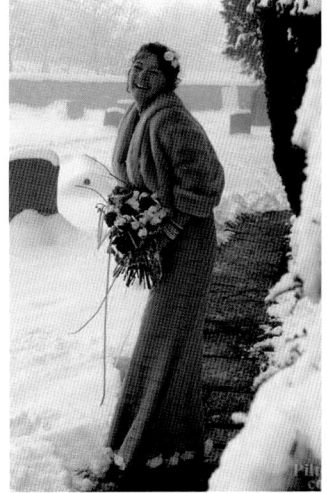

Jasmine Barker's wedding in thick snow at Pylle Church

When the wedding was first planned nobody would have been thinking "Will everyone be able to get there?" but thankfully the weather only stopped a couple of people from making the day and provided lots of great travel adventure stories from those that did.

To ensure the bride got to church on time, Michael Eavis took me, my brother Christian and my two boys Thom and Ollie in a Land Rover to the church, while his wife Liz drove behind in case we broke down!

The service was followed by a reception at Charlton House in Shepton Mallet. Around 50 guests (including many Pilton village locals) attended the reception, making it a very special day.

The snow was so thick that cars had to be left up near the main road that week. I remember walking back down the steep hill by the Chapel after the evening reception, with a full moon, the sparkling snow and silence, after a kind lift home. What is it about snow that makes one want to be a child again? We whooped and giggled, breaking the hanging stillness: it was quite beautiful seeing the village sleeping under the soft mantle of snow, like a clear Alpine night with stars filling the sky, breath making cloudy shapes in the freezing air.

In 2011, a classic example of good neighbourliness happened over at West Compton, as Leonora Clarke recalls:

I bought a big stone ball as a 70th birthday present for a friend in London. It was extremely heavy. I went to London with the ball in the back of the car, en route to work at the Chelsea Flower Show. At about 6.00pm in London, I realised I had left the Chelsea tickets on the dining room table back in West Compton, so decided to get up very early on Sunday morning, drive home and collect them. The ball was still in the car as it was too heavy to lift out. Back at home I ran in, got the tickets, rushed out and opened the back of the car. At this point, the ball decided to leave the car – I could not stop it and did not want it to land on my feet. It bounced out, rolled down the drive, hit the Lindrea's fence, bounced off then set off down the drive, over the road – into the Ballantine's garden. It turned the corner and headed straight for their kitchen door, luckily hitting and breaking a pot on the way, as by now it was moving fast, and I could not stop it. I thought it would go through the door. Lysbeth and Ron were away and it would take some explaining. It ended up on their lawn, where it stayed for several weeks! They were very good about it.

The festival of 2011 had a special 'Spirit of 71' stage to mark the 40th anniversary of the first Glastonbury Fair. Some of the original 49 bands who played then, including the infamous Arthur Brown, played alongside new musicians. It was unfortunately

Trash City vehicles on the move, on the old railway line, unfortunately drowning sounds from nearby stages

situated in an acoustically challenged position, close to the old railway line, along which some of the large recycled machines from Trash City would noisily go, clashing with music from the stage. Those same fantasy machines formed part of the 2012 Paralympics Closing Ceremony.

In 2011, Brown Cow Organics won a top award to add to their vast collection, the Taste of Somerset Harmsworth Award for Outstanding Contribution to Food in Somerset. This is awarded to an individual or company that has put Somerset on the map with inspiration, energy, imagination and use of Somerset ingredients. Brown Cow have certainly done that, for which many congratulations.

In July 2011, the gardens at Burford opened under the National Gardens Scheme for the first time since Christopher and Lindsay Bond took over the house and created exotic gardens based on their foreign travels and restored the woodlands with much replanting and creation of imaginative view points for grandchildren or visitors. In Christopher's own words:

We created a formal and wild garden as a result of the skills of George Windsor, Tony Bailey, Tony Dare and Roger Noble from Pilton and managed the woodlands by making about five miles of tracks through them, replanting with new trees. Robert Kearle and his acrobatic team have done great deeds in developing the woodland.

Michael with his Holstein herd

Another triumph for Worthy Farm in 2011 was to be top out of 68 Holstein herds in Somerset for milk production, which Michael said "for a farmer, is a top accolade." They came fourth in the whole country. The cattle at Worthy Farm are often photographed with the Pyramid behind them but they stay indoors under cover during festival months. In the autumn of 2010, Solarsense installed a large expanse of solar panelling on the "Mootel" to generate electricity, above their smart new cowshed. Solarsense said "It's the first time so many panels have been used on one private installation in Britain, but others are in the concept stage." Measuring 75 metres long by 35 metres wide, it has over 1,100 panels. This should earn the farm a considerable amount over 25 years. It was connected to the grid in October 2010.

In July 2011, Pilton WMC Lamb Cup for skittles, which has been going since 1949, was won by team 'Up the Club.' Linda Tanner was captain, Roger Linthorne took honours for men's highest, while Jean Warry claimed the ladies' prize. Sandra Windsor had ladies' highest score, Nigel Chinnock the men's. They donated their prize money to St Margaret's Hospice in Yeovil.

In early summer 2011, Pilton Cider was first launched on the market. Cider maker, Martin Berkeley features in Alan Stone's recently published book, 'In Search of Cider' from which this extract is taken:

About five years ago, Martin asked Roy Trott, a local farmer, if he could have some apples from a pretty extensive orchard nearby. The first year was very much an amateur communal effort with tubs of apples pounded by sticks to smash them up. The next year he had advanced to a heavy old scratter with a concrete roller.

He obtained a large traditional press with a metre square bed which, despite the disaster of having the metalwork stolen from his garden, he is still using. This is powered by a couple of chunky bottle jacks – though he has now moved on to a modern Speidel mill for the milling.

He and Angela are in the second year of planting out an orchard down the hill at Pylle. With his horticultural background Martin is very interested in some of

the orcharding aspects of cider. Nearly all his apples come from either Pylle or Pilton, as he feels that if using the name *Pilton Cider,* he has to ensure a strong connection between the parish and the product. He mills and presses at his cottage. However, he has now rented premises at the Anglo Brewery in Shepton, where he ferments the juice and carries out the very space consuming functions of bottling and labelling.

Martin Berkeley with new contender in the cider world - Pilton Cider

Martin has focused on producing one upmarket keeved cider product, chasing the holy grail of natural retained sweetness and natural effervescence. Mastering the process has not been without its problems but the cider launched in the early summer of 2011 was excellent.

The apple orchards mentioned are managed by the Orchard Pig, who also advise the village's Gabriel's Orchard. Martin's resulting brew is a sparkling cider, made by the French method, adapting a technique known as 'keeving', popular among French cider-makers. The word probably comes from the French word 'cuvage,' and is a method of making cider that produces a natural sweetness. The cider is made from half-fermented apple juice and needs to be drunk young.

Martin made a career break from computer software and changed from making cider for social pleasure to trying to develop a special taste by traditional methods. For the 2012 Royal Bath and West Show, he commissioned his wife Angela Morley to design and help build the cider bar. In her own words:

I made four large woven willow apples, the largest of which were up to 2.2 metres in diameter, they were set off with a 3.5 metres high bottle of *Pilton Cider.* The stand was certainly original, eye catching and stylish to promote the new season delicious keeved Pilton cider.

Angela Morley with some of her willow sculptures

Although Angela is an artist in willow, she is also an experienced garden designer and horticulturist. During the last 20 years she has run her own business designing gardens and has taught gardening at colleges in Hampshire and Surrey. She works on gardens and commissions across Somerset, Dorset and Hampshire. Angela's designs are characterized by strong, yet simple, structural forms, whilst maintaining an environmentally friendly approach. She builds on her detailed knowledge of plants, ecology, wildlife and woodland management to add richness to her gardens, for both wildlife and the enjoyment of its owners. Her sculptural willow works make original focal points in a garden.

Sadly in May 2012, Pilton Stores closed down and as Nigel and Penny Lane wrote in Roundabout: It is with great regret that we are having to close the village shop, which we have struggled to keep going for 25 years.

Nigel and Penny Lane and family outside the village shop c.2000

When we arrived in Pilton, there were virtually no local supermarkets and buses only ran through the village a few times a week. Since then, the area has been saturated with supermarkets, buses run hourly and more than 200 Piltonians have either died or departed – customers who frequently worked locally, did not own cars and had grown up as regular users of the village shop.

For many years, the Festival has provided a lifeline but withdrawal of their future support has, coupled with the refusal of the bank to further increase a very large overdraft, proved the death knell. Penny and I wish to give special thanks to our few remaining loyal customers and stress how much we will miss our regular contact with them.

2012 saw ongoing preparations for the Queen's Diamond Jubilee, for which a special committee was convened to plan events and fundraising, culminating in a weekend of celebrations in early June. The idea of a national 'Big Lunch' was felt to be the best option. Where better to celebrate than inside the newly restored Tithe Barn?

On Sunday 3rd June 2012, to mark the Queen's Jubilee, there was a morning church service, the bells rang out, then more than 400 people of all ages, dressed in varying degrees of red, white and blue, came to the Tithe Barn for lunch. Long tables were laden with home-made food, as everyone contributed. Michael Eavis had two large banners made specially for the occasion by the Queen's own banner makers, one showing the symbols of the Abbey of Glastonbury, one the Royal Standard, which looked very dramatic hanging from the high roof crucks. Michael was quoted as saying, "It is the first time since we have put the new roof on that the whole village has got together in here to use it. It's a truly great occasion – everyone is here and it's absolutely marvellous."

A large screen was on one wall, projecting the spectacular Thames Jubilee Pageant live from London. There were Bouncy Castles and Punch & Judy for children, plus a Fancy Dress competition for both children and adults. A 'Pied Piper' procession of children playing musical instruments began just as it started raining, but rain failed to stop play. The day continued with a musical evening at the Village Hall, then the following evening a beacon was lit at Burford crossroads as darkness fell, at the time other beacons nationwide were being lit. According to Jim Govier, who together with Sandra Howe, lit the beacon, you could see seven or eight other beacons from up there.

Facing page top row: Groaning table, Punch and Judy audience enthralled, Patriotic cup cakes
2nd row: Rachel, Ben & Pat Rogers having a laugh, "Have you seen my T-shirt?" Mike Case, Rodney Allen on guitar and Anthony Austin on drums lead the musical procession
3rd row: Margaret Wheat, Mugs? Patrick Sumner and Rodney Allen, The Beacon on Monday
Below: Girls love hats, King for a day

Liz Elkin speaks for everyone in her last paragraph:
I really got to know Sandra Howe when we moved back to Pilton in 2006. Sandra was a member of every organisation I joined and, I discovered, others too.

John and Sandra are the driving force behind Pilton Players, Sandra as Chair and actress and John sometimes directing, sometimes writing and always scene shifting. They work together to plan an excellent programme of speakers and entertainment for the Happy Circle, there can't be many of their friends or family members who have not shared their talents with an appreciative audience on a Wednesday afternoon.

Sandra Howe wearing one of her many hats for the Jubilee

If we add secretary of the Playing Fields committee, a role recently relinquished, and a member of the WI it starts to look busy, even for a retired person. And then there are the Flower Show entries! Every year the marquee is full of wonderful crafts and photographs and many of these entries are from the Howe family. Sandra wins competitions locally with her photographs and the competition is tough at home as John takes superb photos too, when he's not fishing or birding.

Sandra has been a long serving Parish Councillor, as was John in his time, and has been Chair of the Council since 2007. She works tirelessly for the Parish and the great success of the Diamond Jubilee Celebrations in the Tithe Barn is due, in no small measure, to Sandra. She chaired the Jubilee Committee but she and John did much of the behind the scenes work which culminated in such a special day. Thank you both.

Artist Candace Bahouth worked on several Jubilee related commissions, one from Clarks in Street, for a commemorative giant desert boot, covered in her intricate mosaic work including many royal images, not forgetting the Corgis.

She made dramatic mirror frames using the same mosaic technique, attracting national attention in a feature of special Jubilee items in a weekend supplement to the Financial Times. She says, "I can be an objective dispassionate admirer of royalty, versus an admiring subject....as an artist and outsider...I think it helps being an American, I can see it all with fresh eyes."

As part of the city of Wells Jubilee celebrations, 60 swans were installed around the city, to mark the 60 years of the Queen's reign. All were decorated differently by artists, schools or community groups. Candace covered hers, sponsored by the Mayor of Wells, entirely with shells. The swans were auctioned for charity, raising a healthy total for local causes. Candace's Queen of Shells was one of the most popular.

In June 2012, a film was released, filmed almost entirely in 2011, entitled 'Glastonbury After Hours: Glastopia' made by documentary film maker, Julien Temple, who had made an earlier film about the Festival. It is set in the 'after hours' part of the Festival, Arcadia, Shangri-La, Strummerville, Block 9 and the Common, which take up seven fields and are certainly radical and alternative, even extreme. A recurring theme is that it is Utopia. Some bright spark is heard to say, "Never heard of it. Is that anywhere near Luton?" Anne Goode would not have been amused, one feels....

Several people commented that most of the bands or music that played at the Jubilee concert outside Buckingham Palace had all appeared on stage at Worthy Farm – the same comments were aired after both Olympics and Paralympics ceremonies. Danny Boyle's dazzling Olympics opening ceremony supposedly included both an abstract version of Glastonbury Tor and a 'mosh pit' similar to the Festival as part of its salute to British culture. The wheel turns full circle.

Sue Green as a child in the 1950s

On a quieter note, Sue Green recalls 60 years of sounds in and around Pilton:

I was delivering the *Roundabout* magazine in 2011 when the A361 was closed except to local traffic. Walking down Park Hill was just as it was when I was a child at Steanbow in the 1950s: quiet and safe. From the age of seven, I was allowed to walk to the village on my own, with these warnings "Don't talk to any tramps" (there were quite a lot) and "don't take a lift from anyone you don't know"(not much traffic anyway). It's so different now: you take your life in your hands walking on that road. The huge lorries make plenty of noise but I also remember that a constant stream of holiday traffic on Friday nights in the 1960s kept my parents awake every week in the holiday season.

Until 1966 a familiar sound was of trains chugging up and down through Park Farm on the Somerset and Dorset line. My father never carried a watch when he worked on Steanbow Farm: if the trains didn't tell him the time, the distant voices that marked playtime at Pilton School told him it was time for morning tea. Now the extensive mechanisation of farm life makes all the noise, or perhaps a helicopter flying overhead but they aren't as deafening as the Hercules planes of ten years or so ago.

Some of the sounds were signs of the seasons: in the 1950s the skylark singing so beautifully but much less common by the time we moved up to Pilton in 1970. There were plenty of cuckoos to disturb the quiet and at one outdoor Rogation Service on the boundary between Pilton and North Wootton they joined in enthusiastically; at times I wished that they would be quiet but I would love to hear them now. The call of buzzards is much more common and we still have birdsong and the dawn chorus to wake us in the mornings.

The Church bells ring out on practice nights and usually on two Sundays each month. 60 years ago Mrs Miell played hymn tunes on the Ellacombe chimes on the other two Sundays of every month.

In the 1970s fortnightly Saturday night discos or groups at the Working Men's Club brought plenty of noise – I know because that was ten yards from my bedroom – but sound-proofing has made that a thing of the past. And, of course, there's the one week in most years when the whole valley is filled with a great variety of rhythmic music.

It's good to be aware of how things were and to value change but most of all to appreciate the sounds of today in the countryside around us and in the sounds of friendship and good neighbourliness in this place that we are privileged to live.

Sue was going to add the tinkling bells of an ice cream van as a sound of yesteryear, only to find that this summer, one was going the rounds again, making the sounds of childhood for new generations.

When I asked Ruth Eavis which of the many village activities with which she is involved stands out in memory, she replied "The Emporium for the Show has always been pretty memorable. It seems to have grown and grown. Many young people have furnished their first homes from it, or stocked their first place while at college. Some small children start collecting very early."

Pilton Show joined the digital age in 2012, the first year that entries could be made in advance online and entry forms printed out, thereby streamlining this process for the Flower Show. Champion fruit and growers from 60 years ago would be well confused, no doubt.

One thing that might confuse farmers from earlier decades is that there are now alpacas or llamas in some fields, as well as sheep and cattle. "Whatever next?" you can hear them saying.

Pilton Show Barn Dance uses colourful bunting made by Frou Frou fashion designer, Cynthia Taylor, who together with husband Barry, organised the Village Supper and Barn Dance for several years. Their role has now been taken over by the Rickwood family

In September 2012, one of Somerset Art Week's regular exhibitors opened her studio. Sukey Erland is well known and respected for her sculptures and also for portraits of people. She has exhibited widely in London and other galleries in the UK, and collectors abroad have also acquired works. Sukey moved to Somerset in 1985, first to North Wootton, then to Pilton where her sister and brother-in-law lived. Bill Appleby, the carpenter, had his workshop next door on the other side, in the old brewery.

When Bill died he left me this fantastic building which I love. Then I was able to have students in for courses. I was *so* glad to leave London.

Sukey Erland with one of her best known sculptures

Before leaving London, she taught sculpture and ceramics. In 1998, she won the John Brandler Prize for Sculpture at the Royal West of England Academy for her study entitled 'Whippets.' Most of her work is cast in bronze or bronze resin, although some is also in stone.

Sukey runs occasional courses in life modelling and drawing at her Malthouse, together with one of her sons Ben, also an artist. A keen supporter of local artists, Sukey has been exhibiting with Somerset Art Weeks since the Open Studios idea began in 1994. Now aged 85, Sukey is still working and her recent passion is for polar bears, groups of mother and cub or cubs, as she declares "I've fallen in love with polar bears at the moment."

Before the bears, her passions have been for otter families of all shapes and sizes, dogs and hares of exquisite shape, horses and a variety of animals and birds, sometimes from mythology, as well as the human form or portraits. She used to keep chickens and horses and sometimes could be seen driving a horse and cart around the village.

In earlier chapters, childhood seemed carefree and carfree: a group of children seem to be enjoying similar freedom, playing with tricycles and toy cars at the Long House corner with Pylle Road, with a parent posted on traffic duty. An image to hold in minds' eye (no camera) is of far too many of them squashed into a battery-run car with two dogs and much laughter. So the spirit of earlier generations lives on, despite modern mechanisation.

Alas, another spirit that everyone hoped would live to see her 100th birthday in December, passed away aged 99 in October. Shiela Perry, mother of Michael, Philip, Patrick and Susan Eavis had a long and full life, the early years of which, mostly before the timescale of these pages, she recorded for her extensive family in a private book of personal memories. Her passing is truly the end of an era.

Charles Johnson, a poet and publisher of poetry, under the former Flarestack Publishing imprint and currently as editor of the long-running 'Obsessed With Pipework' magazine, moved to Abbots Way in 2005. His poem 'Present Participles' says it all:

Learning to live in the present means…

getting barked at by the dog at the stables for taking a walk up Totterdown before breakfast

thinking back seven years to the dash down the M5 from Worcestershire, in a car full of plastic buckets filled with plastic bags full of tropical fish

making new friends every week

trying not to splash as we waded through two inches of muddy water in the exhibits marquee, the year the Pilton Show *almost* got rained off

counting ladybirds hibernating in the belfry

being shown how to plant hanging baskets by the suntanned golfer at the Happy Circle

taking my spade to join the party of bundled neighbours to chip ice back inch by inch off that shoulder where Abbot's Way meets Shutwell Lane below the bus stop

finding myself transported by chamber music in the church

wondering why Daphne my satnav thinks Inkerman Street is still there where they built the Village Hall extension

swapping stories at the Christmas party table

testing the patience of Tracey at the Post Office (and Sally before her) when I insist on pretty stamps for my packages

digging up horseshoes and clay pipestems in the garden

waking up to watch goldfinches and w-o-w (wonder of wonders) a greater spotted woodpecker at the nyger seeds and peanuts in our garden feeder

meeting a deer one morning along Platterwell Lane

being moved by the Vicar's wife, alarmed by Sherlock Holmes and Abanazer, tickled pink by Widow Twanky in the village Christmas plays

abandoning the bike to gather cobwebs in the shed, defeated by the steep Pilton hills

feeling we belong, and

wondering how we ever lived anywhere else.

Illustrations and Picture Credits

Every attempt has been made to trace sources but please let us know any corrections.

Anon 4t, 5, 44b, 61 Hilary Austin 62b, 73, 74, 96t Candace Bahouth 62c. 67, 81t, 86t, 98l, 119, 138-9, 142l, 154, 177 Tony Bailey, 41tr, 48b, 49, 100 Karen Bale 30tl Jasmine Barker 178c, 179cl, bc, 186 Christopher Bond 18, 59, 60, 111r, 174tl Brown Cow Organics 143t Jason Bryant 159l, 163b, 164 Stuart Calff 155bc Daphne Cannock 54t Frank Challener 139bl Ann Cook www.anncookphotos 166-7, 174b Fred Davis/Eric Purchase 105 Jenny de Gex 36, 81b, 84c, 144, 173, 174tr, 179 Jean & Ken Dilkes 137b Margaret Drew 101, 102 Ruth Eavis 71 Liz Elkin 7t, 25t, 30b, 32, 76 Geg Germany 75 Eileen and Jim Govier 83, 107t, 142r, 168 Sally Goldie 114t Sue Green 21tl, c, 111l, 182 Carolyn Griffiths 26, 27, 54b, 55 Linda Heathcoat-Amory 165 The Hewer family 171 Phyllis Higgins 51 Pauline Hobbs 25b, 47 Sandra Howe 144, 169t, 178t, 179 Rob Hurley 3b, 4b, 46 Vaughan Ives 178b Iain Kemp 180b, 181 Chris & Joe King *facing* 1tl, br, 2, 3t, 104 Liz Leyshon 155bl, br Hedley Lomas 16, 161 Ray Loxton 11t, 23, 84b, 107b Mid Somerset News & Media/Shepton Mallet Journal 96b, 124b, 135, 143b, 148, 149, 150, 151, 153, 160, 162b, 169b, 175t Margaret Miles 68, 130 Ann Millard 21b, 25t, 34t, b Totty Milne 42, 127 Angela Morley 176 Charlie Pearce 7b, 12, 37, 41tl, 43, 57 Pilton Cider 176t Pilton Pig 199 Pilton Village History Society *facing* 1bl, 1, 6, 9tl, tr, 50, 106, 115 Ada Plumley 11b Richard Raynsford 180t Bob Scanlon 89 Pauline & Tony Sherwood *facing* 1tr, 41bc, 52,56, 58, 84t, 117, 124t, 128 Ian Sumner 62tl, tr, 69, 87, 91, 108. 114b, 126, 132, 134, 136t, 137t, 140, 141, 144tr, 145, 147, 155t, 158, 159r, 163t, 184 Eileen Taylor 30tr, 41br, 44t, 55b Neil Templar 9b, 10, 19, 20, 29, 172, 183 David Thomas 98r Gavin Thomas 48t Maureen & Steve Tofts 86b, 131 Shannon Turner 97 Brian Walker 64, 65, 96b, 133